SOCIAL WORK AND CRIMINAL JUSTICE:

VOLUME 1

THE IMPACT OF POLICY

Fiona Paterson

Jacqueline Tombs

The Scottish Office Central Research Unit

THE SCOTTISH OFFICE CENTRAL RESEARCH UNIT
1998

The views expressed in this report are those of the
researcher and do not necessarily represent those of the
Department, the Secretary of State for Scotland or The Stationery Office.

SOCIAL WORK AND CRIMINAL JUSTICE
RESEARCH PROGRAMME REPORTS

Paterson, F. and Tombs, J. (1998)

Social Work and Criminal Justice: Volume 1 -
The Impact of Policy. The Stationery Office.

Phase One:

McAra, L. (1998)

Social Work and Criminal Justice: Volume 2 -
Early Arrangements. The Stationery Office.

Phase Two:

Brown, L., Levy, L.
and McIvor, G. (1998)

Social Work and Criminal Justice: Volume 3 -
The National and Local Context. The Stationery Office.

Brown, L., and Levy, L. (1998)

Social Work and Criminal Justice: Volume 4 -
Sentencer Decision Making. The Stationery Office.

McAra, L. (1998a)

Social Work and Criminal Justice: Volume 5 -
Parole Board Decision Making. The Stationery Office.

McIvor, G. and
Barry, M. (1998)

Social Work and Criminal Justice: Volume 6 -
Probation. The Stationery Office.

McIvor, G. and
Barry, M. (1998a)

Social Work and Criminal Justice: Volume 7 -
Community Based Throughcare. The Stationery Office.

CONTENTS

EXECUTIVE SUMMARY

THE POLICY

National Objectives and Standards for Social Work Services in the Criminal Justice System and the 100 per cent funding initiative ('the policy') were introduced in 1991[1] to secure the provision of services which have the confidence of both criminal justice decision makers and the wider public. The development of the policy was informed by the findings from research which identified effective work with offenders.

THE RESEARCH

This report draws on the results of six studies which make up the first two phases of the social research programme designed to evaluate the early stages of policy implementation. The individual studies assess how the policy has been implemented in relation to different aspects of social work services. They cover early arrangements for policy implementation; the national and local context of implementation; advice to the courts and the Parole Board; and probation and throughcare[2]. By discussing the key themes which have emerged from the individual studies, this report both examines the impact of the policy on social work practice and considers the implications of the findings for the longer term.

MAIN POLICY OBJECTIVES

The main objectives of the policy relate to:

the use of custody -

> *to reduce the use of custody in the criminal justice system by increasing the availability, improving the quality and targeting the use of community based court disposals and throughcare services on those most at risk of custody, especially young adult repeat offenders;*

and reducing re-offending -

> *to enable offenders to address their offending behaviour and make a successful adjustment to law-abiding life.[3]*

---

[1] National Standards for Community Service had been introduced in 1989.

[2] Community Service was not included as it had been studied earlier. Services relating to supervised attendance orders, bail and diversion, which have been included in 100% funding since 1992, either permanently or on a pilot basis, are the subject of separate research.

[3] Research Evaluation Strategy Paper, September 1990 (Unpublished).

USE OF CUSTODY

There were mixed research findings about the impact of the policy on reducing the use of custody by the courts and on Parole Board decisions about the release of prisoners:

- Nationally, the use of custody increased slightly during the early stages of policy implementation from 11 per cent of all sheriff court sentences in 1991 to 15 per cent in 1994. However, during the same period the proportion of custodial sentences given for three months or less fell from 61 per cent to 53 per cent.

- In general, social workers were efficiently servicing probation orders and the courts had more confidence in making this disposal.

- The courts viewed the information provided in social enquiry reports (SERs) as useful. The Parole Board were less positive about the information provided in prison social work and home circumstance reports and key information, such as release plans, was often missing.

- The impact of all social work reports, however, was limited by difficulties which social workers had in getting access to reliable information about the circumstances of the current charge and previous offending. Where information was available, social workers tended to use it descriptively rather than to analyse its significance.

- Some areas were found to be targeting services successfully on young offenders at risk of custody. However, young offenders were less likely than adults to be highly motivated to address offending and other problems, less likely to have their risk of re-offending reduced and more likely to breach their probation orders. This means that in areas where social workers are successful in targeting young offenders higher levels of breach and fewer reductions in re-offending risk should be anticipated.

REDUCING RE-OFFENDING

Findings about the impact of the policy on reducing re-offending in the short term showed that:

- There was evidence in relation to both probation and throughcare that social workers and offenders thought that there had been some success in addressing the risk of re-offending.

Longer term follow up of the samples in these studies, which will be undertaken in the third and final phase of this research programme, will provide information on how far effectiveness in addressing the risk of re-offending has been achieved.

INTERMEDIATE POLICY OBJECTIVES

In addition to its longer term objectives, the policy had seven intermediate objectives which were evaluated by the research.

Three of the intermediate objectives were **court-focused:**

> *to improve and strengthen the quality and credibility of community based disposals available to the courts by setting out and securing the implementation of clearly stated Standards and priorities for the provision of these services;*

> *to ensure that the needs of the court are met in terms of an adequate supply of community based disposals of the required quality;*

> *to ensure liaison arrangements exist between the social work department and the courts which are capable of meeting the court needs for social work services.*

A further objective was focused on the concerns of the **Parole Board:**

> *to improve the quality of statutory supervision of released prisoners so as to encourage earlier release on licence and compliance with licence requirements. To improve the quality of voluntary supervision provided to released prisoners by social work departments.*

One objective was targeted at a **specific group of offenders:**

> *to ensure the development of services specifically aimed at those at increased risk of custody, especially young adult offenders.*

The last two objectives were concerned with **social work organisation:**

> *to ensure that organisation, management and delivery of services are efficient and effective;*

> *to ensure that the provision and use of services are monitored to establish the extent to which the initiative's objectives are being met.*

The extent to which the intermediate policy objectives have been realised is summarised below.

The Court

Research on the impact of the policy on social work services to the courts found that the policy has had a positive effect on the judiciary's view of social work services. A major effort has been made to improve liaison with the judiciary and this has helped to promote a better understanding of what social work can provide. Sentencers were satisfied with the Standards to which SERs were generally written and now expressed confidence that community disposals will be thoroughly administered and supervised. Their confidence was largely borne out by the findings of the research on probation.

However, on a number of key issues the research identified a need for further progress. The National Standards require clear links to be made between individual offending and social circumstances. The research did not find that these links were being made. The information provided by social workers about offenders' social, family and employment characteristics was found to predominate over information about their offending. SERs tended to describe rather than analyse information about offenders. Thus, even where information was presented, it was not always linked together to provide a basis for assessing risk of re-offending. As a result, risk of re-offending was rarely assessed and this affected the credibility of proposals for services which could contribute to reducing that risk.

Inadequate access to verified information about the offence often created difficulties for social workers preparing social enquiry reports. However, difficulties with social enquiry reports were also, on occasion, associated with resistance on the part of social workers to the offence focused approach which the Standards are promoting.

The National Standards relating to probation promote a focus on addressing offending and, overall, probation practice was being re-focused in this way. However, the extent to which offending was a direct focus was variable across the areas studied. Where the Standards were less often met, social workers were more likely to undertake work focused on relationships, use of leisure time and physical or mental health. In contrast, social workers working more closely to the Standards were more likely to undertake work focused on offending, drug or alcohol misuse, employment and financial problems.

Some elements of the Standards which are aimed at contributing to increased effectiveness of work with offenders were not always being fully used. This was the case, for example, with action plans which should outline the work to be undertaken during probation orders. Action plans are a means through which clear and explicit expectations can be communicated to offenders. However, some offenders receiving probation were not aware of the existence of an action plan or what it contained.

The policy has encouraged the development of specialist criminal justice social work services, though specialisation by individuals within criminal justice social work was less apparent. Most social workers were providing a broad range of services within the context of probation and only a small number of specialist resources was available within the study areas. These included intensive probation, sex offender programmes, domestic violence programmes, substance misuse and mental health services, employment and supported accommodation. There is scope for further development of specialist resources and, particularly in rural areas, for the development of models of service delivery which will take account of the small numbers of offenders and the variable levels of demand.

Parole Board

Overall there was mixed evidence about the extent to which National Standards were being implemented in relation to the provision of information to the Parole Board and services for throughcare. This means that the impact of the policy on performance and outcome in these areas has not been fully tested.

The research on parole and throughcare identified that communication needed to be improved between Parole Board members, community social workers and prison social workers. Members of the Parole Board generally wanted more information about social work policy and services and social workers wanted more specific feedback about the outcomes of parole considerations.

As a result of limited communication, Parole Board members, offenders, and social workers had different understandings about the contribution of social work to throughcare. Thus the Board looked to prison social work to address the risk of re-offending and understood that community based throughcare was providing supervision or was focusing on re-integration into the community. Ex-prisoners were seeking help with their social and other circumstances. Like the Parole Board, they thought that the issue of offending had been addressed by or within prison and that social work concerns about re-offending after release were irrelevant. However, consistent with the approach promoted in the Standards, community social workers focused on individual ex-prisoners' responsibility to address offending.

While there appeared to be liaison arrangements within particular social work departments between local community and prison social workers, no arrangements were found to be in place for liaison with prison social workers in other local authorities. This limited communication about the preparation and content of reports. Prison and community social workers did not agree about who should take responsibility for developing release plans; one result of this was that fewer than half of the reports in the sample had release plans.

Prison social work and home circumstances reports to the Parole Board were found to have had a minimal impact on decisions. Their impact may have been limited because of patchy information on risk of re-offending and the tendency to describe rather than to assess the significance of the information provided. As with SERs, there were difficulties with access to verified information about the offence and this meant that reports were not necessarily being prepared on as reliable a basis as the Standards are promoting.

The Standards promote the use of a release plan in order to communicate clearly to the Parole Board and to ex-prisoners what the objectives of throughcare services will be and how they are to be met. However, most ex-prisoners were not aware of these plans. Further, the Standards for contacts with prisoners following release were met in only around half of the sample. For this reason the research found that the framework for throughcare set out in the Standards was less well used than was the framework for probation.

Young Offenders

The target group for this policy - young offenders at high risk of custody - posed particular difficulties for probation and the development of services specifically aimed at this group was uneven across the study areas.

Younger offenders were less likely to have been motivated to address offending and other problems, were slightly less likely to have demonstrated some reduction in risk of re-offending, and were three times as likely as adults to have breached their probation orders. The area with the highest proportion of young offenders at high risk of custody was also most likely to have negative outcomes to probation. This indicates that, to the extent that there is effective targeting of offenders at whom the policy is directed, a higher level of breach needs to be anticipated.

More generally, this illustrates the importance of setting service outcome indicators which are appropriate for particular groups of offenders. There are, however, difficulties for local authorities in setting these levels because of the absence of information on patterns of recidivism at national level.

Social Work Organisation

The main forum for national consultation, the Main Consultation Group (MCG), set the tone for policy implementation. The composition of the MCG reflects the prominence which has, to date, been given to court focused services. While the MCG has therefore been effective in promoting communication with the courts, communication with the Parole Board and Scottish Prison Service (SPS), who are not represented on the MCG, has been less effective.

At a local level relationships between sentencers, the independent sector and social workers were thought to be good. On the other hand, liaison with prison social workers, other than on a formal basis within individual authorities, and routine monitoring of prison social work, was less satisfactory.

CONCLUSION

The National Objectives and Standards and the 100% funding initiative are informed by an understanding of what constitutes effective practice with offenders and mark a significant shift in the approach of social work to offending. The Social Work (Scotland) Act 1968 gave social work departments a legal duty to promote social welfare. The interpretation of the principle of promoting welfare which was subsequently adopted meant that what became known as *offender services*, became part of generic social work. Thus the model of practice involved a focus on individual welfare as the primary concern and offending behaviour as a secondary issue. We characterise this as the **welfare model**.

The current policy marks a change in emphasis: individual responsibility for offending behaviour should now be the primary focus of social work and welfare issues are of secondary consideration. Organisationally this has involved the development of what are now known as *criminal justice social work services* based on what we characterise as a **responsibility model** of practice. In contrast to the welfare model, which sees offending behaviour as primarily a response to personal and social circumstances, the responsibility model recognises both that offenders make active choices in their behaviour and that choice is always situated within a person's particular social and personal context.

In the shorter term most of the major structural changes to organisation and management necessary to facilitate specialist criminal justice social work services have been set in place. In the longer term full implementation of the policy will require fundamental cultural changes within social work practice. Professional cultural changes, that is changes in the routine understanding and practice of individual social workers, so that the responsibility model comes to be understood and broadly accepted as 'good practice', take much longer to establish.

The research found that some of the required structural changes had not yet happened: detailed links between social work and criminal justice agencies were not fully operational. For example, there were difficulties with social work access to verified information about offending. The significance of this access not being in place is that it is only very recently, and associated with the new policy, that social workers have been expected to have anything to say directly about criminal behaviour in individual cases. The research found, however, that even where verified information was available, social workers did not always make use of it. Indeed, some social workers showed unwillingness to access individual social work records without prisoner agreement. More often than not, the information within social work reports was characteristic of the welfare rather than the offence-focused responsibility model of social work practice.

This illustrates some of the factors which inhibit full realisation of a key shift required by the policy: from social workers as experts in welfare to the production of a new kind of social work expertise - an expertise in risk assessment to assist with the targeting of organisational resources and to indicate their potential to impact on criminal behaviour. While the policy has moved beyond the initial stages of implementation, it is still at an early stage in making progress towards achieving the long term objectives of establishing criminal justice social work services and practice which will be effective in reducing the risk of custody, where appropriate, and the risk of re-offending. The policy is in the process of refocusing the contribution of social work in this area from a primary concern with the welfare of individual offenders to the requirements of criminal justice.

PART 1

IMPACT OF THE POLICY

CHAPTER ONE

SOCIAL WORK AND CRIMINAL JUSTICE

INTRODUCTION

This report evaluates the impact of central government policy to set National Objectives and Standards for Social Work Services in the Criminal Justice System (National Standards) and to provide 100 per cent of the funding to the local authorities responsible for these services (the 100 per cent funding initiative). The National Standards were introduced in 1991[4] at the same time as the 100 per cent funding initiative. These are complementary elements of current social work policy in Scotland ('the policy') which aims to secure the provision of effective services which have the confidence of both criminal justice decision-makers and the wider public.

The report draws on the results of six studies which make up the first two phases of a social research programme which is evaluating policy implementation. By discussing the key themes which have emerged from the individual studies, the report examines the impact of the policy on social work practice and considers the implications of the findings for the longer term.

In the first chapter we set the context for the report by outlining the research programme and the policy objectives. We describe the way in which the policy deals with different types of risk associated with offending and changing models of social work practice. Finally, we provide a brief description of the points of contact between social work and criminal justice.

CONTEXT

The Research Programme

The policy has been subject to ongoing review and evaluation since its introduction. This includes a programme of inspection by the Social

---

4   National Standards for Community Service had been introduced two years earlier in 1989. Research on community service was undertaken at that time. This studied 12 Scottish schemes and followed through a sample of 134 offenders to identify any re-convictions. It was found that 40% had been reconvicted within 12 months and were most likely to have further convictions for public order offences or dishonesty. Offenders who found community service to be a very worthwhile experience were slightly less likely to be re-convicted than other offenders. McIvor, G (1989) *An Evaluative Study of Community Service by Offenders in Scotland*, Social Work Research Centre, University of Stirling; McIvor, G (1992) *Reconviction Among Offenders Sentenced to Community Service*, Social Work Research Centre, University of Stirling.

Work Services Inspectorate (SWSI)[5], interpretation of statistics and a programme of social research. The programme of social research is being conducted in three phases; it began in 1993 and will continue until 1998 when the third and final phase will be complete.

The main purpose of the study in the first phase was to examine the responses of key criminal justice decision-makers and Scottish Office officials to the principal objectives of the policy and the early arrangements for its implementation[6]. The main aims of the second phase have been to assess policy implementation and the extent to which it has resulted in achievement of the policy objectives.

Five studies have been conducted in phase two:

- a study of the national and local arrangements for policy implementation;

- a study of sentencer decision making which examined the way in which the policy has affected social enquiry reports, a key method of communicating with the courts;

- a study of probation services has assessed changes in social work probation practice;

- a study of Parole Board decision making has examined the way in which the policy has affected home circumstance and prison social work reports, key methods of communicating with the Parole Board;

- a study of changes in social work practice in relation to throughcare[7].

Details of the studies and summaries of their findings are provided in Part Two of this report. The final phase of the research programme will focus on longer term outcomes.

The research has been carried out in four areas, which are referred to as Scott, Wallace, Burns and Bruce. The areas include urban and rural locations and were selected to reflect a range of social work organisational arrangements and different levels of use of custodial disposals by the local courts.[8] Characteristics of the areas are outlined in Table 1.1.

---

[5] *Achieving National Standards* published by SWSI in 1993. Three further inspections have reported more recently: *'Helping the Courts Decide'*, 1996; *Realistic and Rigorous*, (1996); and *A Positive Penalty*, (1997). These are concerned with social enquiry reports and community service.

[6] See McAra, L. (1998) *Social Work and Criminal Justice: Early Arrangements*. Local authorities were not included in this study because of the inspection which was being undertaken at that time.

[7] Community service had been studied earlier. See McIvor, G. (1992) *Sentenced to Serve: The Operation and Impact of Community Service by Offenders*, Aldershot: Avebury.

[8] More detail about their characteristics is given in Annex 1.

Table 1.1: Characteristics of the Study Areas

	Area Type	Court Features
Scott	Large town bordering urban area.	Large court. Above national average use of custody, community service and probation. Below average use of fines.
Wallace	City.	Large court. Above national average use of custody, community service and probation. Below average use of fines.
Burns	Large town in rural area.	Medium court. Below national average use of custody, about average use of community service and fines, above average use of probation.
Bruce	Small town in rural area.	Small court. Below national average use of custody and fines, above average use of community service and probation.

Scott and Wallace were in urban areas and had large courts with an above national average use of custody. Burns and Bruce were in rural areas with smaller courts where the use of custody was below the national average[9]. All courts in the study areas had a higher use of probation than the national average.

The research has been undertaken early in the life of the policy and to some extent results reflect the dynamic of the implementation process as well as the impact of the policy itself. The detailed review arrangements for the policy have meant that early implementation has also involved a process of adjustment and development of policy detail as information about aspects of its impact has become available. Nevertheless, though there have been adjustments in emphasis, fundamental features of the policy, for example, its objectives, have not been subject to change.

The Policy

National Standards and the 100 per cent funding initiative were developed in the context of a recognition that Scotland has a high use of imprisonment and that prisons may not be the most appropriate environment in which to deal with less serious offenders. The Government's policy and concern about the use of custody were set out in November 1988 by the then Secretary of State[10].

---

[9] For a fuller discussion see Brown. L, and Levy. L, (1998) *Social Work and Criminal Justice: Sentencer Decision Making.*

[10] Malcolm Rifkind speaking at the Kenneth Younger Memorial Lecture to the Howard League for Penal Reform (Scotland).

'Prisons are both expensive to build and to run and do not provide the ideal environment in which to teach an offender how to live a normal and law abiding life, to work at a job or to maintain a family. If offenders can remain in the community, under suitable conditions, they should be able to maintain their family ties, opportunities for work or training and they may be better placed to make some reparation for their offence.' (National Standards Part 1 para 2)

More recent statements have been consistent with the continuation of this concern. For example, the l996 White Paper on Crime and Punishment notes "...The Government remains committed to the provision of a range of non-custodial sentences sufficient to enable the courts to use alternatives to custody where appropriate to the offence and consistent with the primary focus of custody on public protection.' (paragraph 9.1) Reviewing the high percentage of short custodial sentences still passed in Scotland in 1994 when 83 per cent were for less than six months, the White Paper states 'These figures raise questions about the use of custody and whether more can be done to shake out of the prison system those who do not need to be there.' (paragraph 10.3)

The purpose of the policy is to strengthen the non-custodial sentences already available to the courts in order to reduce the use of custody by making effective services available.

"5. ......The overall aim is to create a situation in which it is practicable to use prisons as sparingly as possible through providing community based disposals which contain and reduce offending behaviour, assist social integration, have the confidence of the courts and the wider public, and make efficient and effective use of available resources.

6. Another important aim is to help released prisoners settle into the community and minimise the risk of their re-offending......" (National Standards, Part 1; paras 5 - 6)

The main objectives of the policy are to:

"reduce the use of custody in the criminal justice system by increasing the availability, improving the quality and targeting the use of community based court disposals and throughcare services on those most at risk of custody, especially young adult repeat offenders;

enable offenders to address their offending behaviour and make a successful adjustment to law abiding life." (Research Evaluation Strategy Paper, September 1990)

A number of intermediate objectives need to be met in order for there to be progress in achieving the main objectives. The intermediate policy objectives are:

• "To improve and strengthen the quality and credibility of community based disposals available to the courts by setting out and securing the implementation of clearly stated Standards and priorities for the provision of these services;

- to ensure that the needs of the court are met in terms of an adequate supply of community based disposals of the required quality;

- to ensure the development of services specifically aimed at those at increased risk of custody, especially young adult offenders;

- to ensure liaison arrangements exist between the social work department and the courts which are capable of meeting the court needs for social work services;

- to improve the quality of statutory supervision of released prisoners so as to encourage earlier release on licence and compliance with licence requirements;

- to improve the quality of voluntary supervision provided to released prisoners by social work departments;

- to ensure that organisation, management and delivery of services is efficient and effective;

- to ensure that the provision and use of services are monitored to establish the extent to which the initiative's objectives are being met."

(Research Evaluation Strategy Paper, September 1990)

The research evaluation examines the extent to which these objectives have been met.

The 100 per cent funding initiative and National Standards were first applied to community service in 1989 and, following the 1990 Law Reform (Miscellaneous Provisions) (Scotland) Act, were extended in 1991 to: the preparation of social enquiry reports and associated court services; probation; and throughcare (the provision of social work services to offenders in custody and on release). Since then, the initiative has been extended to bail schemes[11] on a pilot basis, supervised release orders[12] and supervised attendance orders[13]. It is intended to include

---

[11] Bail schemes are to enable the court to make more use of bail. They involve bail information and accommodation officers providing verified information to the court about those eligible for bail and providing accommodation for those who would otherwise lack a suitable address. More recently schemes have been extended to provide supervision of those given bail.

[12] These were introduced under Section 209 of the Criminal Procedure (Scotland) Act 1995. A court when passing sentence of at least one and less than four years may make a supervised release order requiring the person to be under supervision for up to 12 months on release from custody.

[13] Introduced under Section 62 of the Law Reform (Miscellaneous Provisions) (Scotland) Act 1990 and amended by the Criminal Justice (Scotland) Act 1995. The supervised attendance order was introduced as an alternative to custody for fine defaulters requiring them to participate in constructive activities as instructed by the supervising officer.

diversion from prosecution in the 100 per cent funding arrangement, subject to the progress of pilot schemes. At present, fine supervision, means enquiry and deferred sentence supervision are not included in the funding initiative.

THE POLICY, RISK AND SOCIAL WORK PRACTICE

Policy on social work criminal justice services is an important part of wider policy relating to criminal justice. By providing services which assist offenders to address their offending behaviour, social work has an important role to play in supporting Government aims for criminal justice. A concern with risk is fundamental to social work criminal justice policy and this is reflected in the importance of risk assessment which, consistent with the major policy objectives, has focused on risk of custody and risk of re-offending. Addressing these risks is the purpose of a second major element of the policy, that of changing social work practice.

Risk

Over the period of implementing the 100 per cent funding initiative the priorities for criminal justice policy have been to prevent crime, to protect the public, to assist victims and, without prejudicing these priorities, to replace custodial with non-custodial disposals, where appropriate. Criminal justice policy priorities therefore include a concern with a third kind of risk: risk to the public. By looking at criminal justice and social work perspectives on risk we also illustrate a difference in perspectives on offending.

Risk To The Public

Risk to the public arises from people's behaviour and its impact on other people. Sometimes it is used to refer specifically to the dangers of violence, though it can also include concerns about a wider range of harms. Decisions about how the criminal justice system should react to risks are not simply based on responses to offenders but are also based on notions of public interest.

Generally "public interest" encompasses the idea that people should act within the law to ensure that both the public and the process of justice are protected from criminal behaviour and that those accused of criminal behaviour are innocent unless their own admission or a fair trial establishes their guilt. Most criminal justice practitioners see themselves as working in the public interest by operating a system of criminal justice which is concerned with the protection of the public.

Protection of the public is a fundamental principle informing the administration of the criminal law and is referred to in criminal justice practitioners' accounts of the significance of the risks which are posed by offenders in individual cases. There is, as some have noted, sometimes a tension within criminal justice created by the co-existence of notions of proportionality in response to criminal behaviour which has been proved (seriousness) and the need to protect the public from risk potentially posed by future (and therefore unproved) behaviour (dangerousness)[14].

Risk to the public received limited attention within social work criminal justice policy at the time of the research. For example, while there are a number of terms used within the National Standards which refer to protection of the public, the significance of this concept is not developed[15]. The reason for this was that risk to the public was subsumed within risk of re-offending and this has meant that the implications of public risk have not been systematically addressed within the policy.

Risk Of Custody

The risk of custody is about the chance that the criminal justice system will respond to offending by imposing or, in the case of the Parole Board, continuing a custodial sentence. The risk of custody is dependent not simply on the nature of an offence, and the sentencer's response to the offence which resulted in conviction, but also upon the range of existing sentencing options, for example, whether there are suitable intensive probation or community service schemes available. Although the criminal justice system is constitutionally separate from government, Government policy on service provision gives shape and detail to the options available to the criminal justice system when taking action and, in particular, to the courts when sentencing.

Risk of custody is of limited concern to criminal justice practitioners. It is, however, a major concern of the policy which has as a key objective the reduction of the use of custody, where appropriate, by increasing the availability, improving the quality and targeting the use of community based court disposals and throughcare services on those most at risk of custody.

---

[14] See, for example, Nash, M. (1992) 'Dangerousness Revisited'; *International Journal of the Sociology of Law*, 20:337-349. Also see Brown, M. (1996) 'Serious Offending and the Management of Public Risk in New Zealand' in *British Journal of Criminology* 36, 1: 18-36.

[15] There are a number of terms within the National Standards which are directly relevant to public protection: public protection/safety; social harm; risk to the community; risk to agency; public interest. These cover 14 references, one of which is to the Secretary of State's 1988 speech to the Howard League; five refer to government policy in the criminal justice system or to the operation of that system. Only eight of the 14 references are directly linked with social work services: six of these relate to throughcare or to special categories of offender, such as offenders against children and sex offenders, and two refer to alerting agencies to the possible risks posed by offenders.
Following the research reported here SWSI have drawn attention to the need to address risk to the public more systematically (SWSI, 1996)

Risk Of Re-Offending

Risk of re-offending is the risk that offenders will repeat the behaviour or engage in other behaviour which breaches the criminal law. This risk is of direct concern to the criminal justice system and is also reflected in one of the principal objectives of the policy which is to enable offenders to address their offending behaviour and make a successful adjustment to law abiding life.

Risk of re-offending is both about people's behaviour and the criminal justice system's response to that behaviour. While the discussion of re-offending within the National Standards acknowledges that social work practice is dealing with both of these elements, the potential for tension between the social work and the criminal justice response to offending behaviour is not discussed. The criminal justice system operates with an understanding of crime as being the responsibility of individuals who are culpable because they have choice. However, the understanding of crime embedded in social work practice has generally been that adverse circumstances can precipitate criminal behaviour. Accordingly, the response to crime has been to provide offenders with assistance to tackle the personal and social difficulties which underlie their offending. We refer to this as the 'welfare model'. This model of social work practice does not always sit easily with the public protection concerns which often guide the criminal justice system's response to offenders.

Thus, social work responses to individual offenders are not necessarily the same as criminal justice responses which, in addition to concerns about public protection, take into account matters such as public opinion and deterrence. As we shall argue, the tensions between social work and criminal justice perspectives and their associated responses to crime have consequences for the impact of the policy.

Social Work Practice: From Welfare to Responsibility

The Standards have begun to address the difference in social work and criminal justice perspectives by promoting a shift from a welfare model of practice to a model in which social work practice is focused on the responsibility of offenders for their behaviour (responsibility model).

The welfare model emerged, in part, as a consequence of the Social Work (Scotland) Act 1968[16]. This Act gave social work departments a legal duty to promote social welfare[17] while at the same time integrating probation and aftercare services (which became known as "offender

---

[16] Underpinned by the 'Kilbrandon Philosophy' the Act followed from the 1964 *Report of the Kilbrandon Committee on Children and Young Persons (Scotland)* HMSO. The Act instituted the welfare based Children's Hearing System to deal both with children who offend and those in need of care and protection, thereby removing children (defined as those under 16) in trouble from the criminal courts (with few exceptions).

[17] See the preamble to the Social Work (Scotland) Act 1968 and Part II section 12 (1) of the Act.

services") within a broader social work department. In so doing, it instituted social work practice based on teams of generic social workers working to promote the social welfare of clients through individual casework.

Many generic social workers did not have the specialist skills required for work with offenders and this led to a degree of scepticism amongst criminal justice practitioners about the potential contribution of social work - seeing it as centred on the needs of the client/offender rather than on the wider public protection concerns of the court (e.g. Moody and Tombs 1982; Moore and Wood 1992). Local authorities had to fund offender services out of their general income, thus these services were in competition for resources with other local authority services. As a result, they were not always of sufficient quantity and quality to meet the requirements of the courts.

The remedy for the gap in social work credibility and expertise has been the National Standards which are a means of promoting dedicated social work criminal justice practice. The remedy for the problem of resources has been the 100% funding initiative which refunds to local authorities the full approved cost of most social work criminal justice services.

National Standards set a framework for providing services to the criminal justice system by codifying the elements of the approach to service provision and practice which the policy is promoting. In contrast to the welfare model, which sees offending behaviour as primarily a response to personal and social circumstances, the responsibility model recognises both that offenders make active choices in their behaviour and that choice is always situated within a person's particular social and personal context. The Standards contain a practice supplement[18] based on research findings on the characteristics of effective interventions with offenders. This supplement is intended to inform the development of professional social work criminal justice practice and its management. The model of social work within the Standards is premised on the view that, through social work intervention which promotes individual responsibility for behaviour together with social responsibility for alleviating adverse circumstances, offending will be discouraged. Importantly, in contrast to the notion of individual responsibility associated with the public protection principles which inform criminal justice, the responsibility model contains elements of both individual and social responsibility.

Nevertheless, social work authorities continue to have a statutory duty to

---

[18] A Supplement to the National Objectives and Standards for Social Work Services in the Criminal Justice System (1991) The Scottish Office Social Work Services Group. In this respect the comment, made in relation to the Standards for England and Wales, that they *are more concerned with consistency and compliance than with effectiveness* (Raynor, P. Gelsthorpe, L. and Tisi, A. (1995), 'Quality Assurance, Pre-Sentence Reports and the Probation Service', *British Journal of Social Work*, 25: 483) is not relevant to Scotland.

promote social welfare, therefore the policy is being implemented within an organisational context which remains underpinned by social welfare considerations. This means that there is still a potential for tension with the public interest ethos of the criminal justice system. In 1991 the compatibility of criminal justice and social work approaches was asserted by SWSG following an analysis of social work values and their compatibility with the requirements of criminal justice:

> "...It will be for local authorities to ensure that they pursue the achievement of national objectives for social work services in the criminal justice system within the overall context of social work, in compliance with the National Standards and taking account of the concerns of sentencers and criminal justice agencies." (O'Leary 1991[19])

The policy has meant that social work departments have become more accountable to central government for the link between finance and services and to the courts for the link between services and sentencing requirements. As part of this process we are witnessing the refinement of the machinery through which social work is held accountable for its contribution to criminal justice.

At one level the changes are about improving service efficiency and effectiveness. But the particular version of efficiency and effectiveness promoted within the policy and the way this shapes the content of social work involves, as we have noted, a fundamental shift in social work boundaries and a changing understanding of the professional contribution of social work to criminal justice. Language is, of course, a key signifier of these processes - thus we now talk about objectives and Standards, performance and outcome indicators, programmes of work with offenders not guidance and individual casework with clients.

Social Work and the Criminal Justice Process

There are a number of points in the criminal justice process when social work can potentially have an influence. These are:

- when the procurator fiscal is deciding whether a case should be dealt with through the criminal justice system or diverted from it, the availability of diversion schemes can have an influence;

- if the case proceeds to court, then, when the procurator fiscal and the court are each deciding their views about pre-trial release on bail or remand in custody, the availability of bail information, accommodation and supervision services can influence the decision.

---

[19] A draft statement of values was considered by SWSG in 1990/91. The quotation has been taken from 'Summary of the Main Principles Adopted by Central Government in the Preparation of the National Standards Document.', paper presented by SWSG's Senior Social Work Adviser to a Seminar for Local Authority Managers in March, 1991.

If a person is remanded then the court social worker will assess whether they are at risk of self-harm;

- when the court is considering whether the appropriate sentence would be custody or a community based disposal such as community service, probation, or a monetary penalty, social enquiry reports[20] provide a means of informing the court both about the offender and about the social work services which would be available for particular sentence options;

- after sentence, if there is default on a fine, social work services can report on the suitability of a supervised attendance order as an alternative to prison;

- spanning the period in custody and after release, social work can provide throughcare services[21] for offenders directed towards their reintegration into the community. **At the point of custodial sentence** the court social worker will identify practical problems, advise about prison social work services and assess whether the person is at risk of self harm; **in prison** social work can provide services to motivate prisoners to examine their offending behaviour and to develop pre- and post-release plans; **for the Parole Board**, social work can provide reports on the impact of custody on the offender and on the home circumstances to which an offender would be returning on release; and **following release** social work provides services and advice to ex-prisoners on request, or supervision as a condition of release on order or licence.

Social work can therefore affect decisions made by prosecutors, sentencers and members of the Parole Board and the views of these decision makers have been taken into account within policy development. However, it is sentencers who are most frequently the recipients of social work information and views and therefore the focus of policy implementation has been primarily towards the judiciary.

CONCLUSION

Informed by a particular understanding of what constitutes effective practice with offenders, the National Objectives and Standards and the 100 per cent funding initiative mark a change in approach of social work to offending. Risk to the public, a major criminal justice concern, has not

---

[20] As well as social enquiry reports (SERs), social workers provide oral and stand down reports which provide specific information which may make it possible for the court to deal with a case without requesting an SER, or to continue a case on bail rather than to remand in custody, or to suggest that an SER or other report might be helpful. Pre-trial and supplementary reports are also provided by social workers. For a fuller description of social work services to the criminal justice system see Brown. L, and Levy. L, 1998.

[21] For a fuller outline of throughcare services see McIvor. G, and Barry. M, (1997a) *Social Work and Criminal Justice: Community Based Throughcare.*

featured prominently within the policy which has focused on risk of custody and of re-offending. By promoting a shift from a welfare model of practice to a responsibility model in which social work practice is focused on the responsibility of offenders for their behaviour, the policy is addressing the difference in social work and criminal justice perspectives on responses to criminal behaviour.

In the next chapter we outline the mechanisms through which the policy has been implemented at both national and local level. In Chapter Three we begin our analysis of the influence of the policy on social work views and practice as well as on criminal justice decision makers. We look at the ways in which social work services try to shape judicial understanding and to influence sentencing practice by the provision of social enquiry reports to sentencers. The ways in which the risk of re-offending are addressed through the provision of probation services are also considered. In Chapter Four we examine the contribution of social work to the work of the Parole Board and to the supervision of ex-prisoners subject to throughcare. Finally, in Chapter Five, we consider the progress which has been made towards achievement of policy objectives, some of the practical outcomes of policy implementation and the implications of findings for social work and criminal justice relations.

CHAPTER TWO

NATIONAL POLICY AND LOCAL CONTEXT

INTRODUCTION

Successful policy implementation requires criminal justice and social work agencies to communicate well with each other and to work together, as this will support effective work with offenders. Recognising the importance of this, the government established consultation and liaison mechanisms at a national and local level. The purpose of this chapter is to describe the process of policy consultation at national level, comment on the significance of the contributions and look briefly at the local context of the services examined in this report. Unless otherwise indicated, this chapter draws on the findings of *Social Work and Criminal Justice: The National and Local Context* (Brown, L., Levy, L. and McIvor, G. 1998). A full account of the methods used is provided in the study report[22].

NATIONAL POLICY DEVELOPMENT

At a national level a Main Consultation Group (MCG) was established in 1989 to review social work criminal justice services and to oversee the production of the original National Objectives and Standards. The membership of the MCG at that time included central government, local authorities, the judiciary, the police, professional social work and the voluntary sector. Subgroups, responsible for developing particular sections of the Standards, were drawn from organisations contributing to the MCG and the universities. For the purposes of policy implementation, criminal justice representatives only included the courts and police. The Scottish Prison Service and the Parole Board were not represented on the Group[23]. As we shall see, the composition of the MCG has been reflected in the focus of service development which has been on social work services to the courts, with communication and inter-agency working remaining limited in the parole and throughcare of prisoners where services have been less developed.

Main Consultation Group

The MCG's role is to advise the Secretary of State for Scotland about the translation of policy into practice. Since the National Standards were introduced in 1991, the MCG has been responsible for overseeing the

---

[22] Interviews were conducted with representatives of the MCG and local authority managers; MCG documents and local authority plans and policy documents were analysed.

[23] Membership now includes the Scottish Prison Service.

review and revision of Standards in the light of experience. The Group has been an important vehicle for fostering liaison at a national level and has set the tone for localised implementation of the policy. Representatives of the Group who were interviewed saw its current main function as being to monitor the development of the Standards. Since Group members bring to it their own professional and organisational contexts and the associated understandings of issues, the MCG provides a forum in which those from different perspectives can develop a broad overview. MCG interviewees agreed that the Group had been particularly effective in bringing together a range of practical experience and views.

However, interviewees also thought that, in practice, it had not been possible for the MCG to achieve its objective of overseeing the progress of National Standards' implementation and therefore to realise its potential for taking a strategic overview. There were two reasons for this. First, the pattern of annual meetings was seen by MCG interviewees as limiting the Group to receiving progress reports on the implementation of the Standards, impeding the possibility of building up momentum and restricting the development of relationships among members[24]. Second, MCG interviewees were uncertain about the status of some views given in meetings by MCG members from the voluntary sector and the judiciary. They were unsure whether the views were representative of a range of experience across Scotland, or reflected the perspective of the individuals concerned, since these members do not work within contexts where there are established organisational mechanisms for routine consultation and representation.

MCG interviewees saw the Group as having been successful in its main work but thought that the price of this success had been the avoidance of areas of potential disagreement. They said that if potentially contentious areas were raised within the Group, the response was to block if there was a problem, so that an issue would be remitted for consideration elsewhere. There were sensitivities within the Group and interviewees noted that initially trust had to be established among its members. In part, sensitivities reflected the different roles of Group members: central government, responsible for the policy and for funding; the local authorities, responsible for services; and the judiciary, constitutionally independent, responsible for sentencing and consequently the use made of services. Given these different roles, it was not surprising that the consensus reached on how best to progress the policy, was fragile.

---

[24] The minutes of the November 1993 meeting of the Main Consultation Group indicate that the question of more frequent meetings was raised but that the members at that time decided to continue to meet on an annual basis.

The Relationship Between Social Work and Criminal Justice

A fundamental theme of policy implementation is the contribution of social work to broader criminal justice aims. This theme resonated in the responses which MCG interviewees gave to questions about their respective professions and roles in the Group. Their references to the three types of risk (to the public; of re-offending; of custody) described in Chapter One, reflected the difference between the role of the decision makers (the judiciary) and that of the service providers (social work departments). Both social work and judicial MCG members were agreed that the distinction between social work and judicial concerns about offending was crucial. Social workers were not advising the courts on sentencing and could not take into account matters, such as deterrence and public reaction, which the court would need to take account of in reaching a decision. They saw the role of local authorities as being to develop services for offenders released by the court to the community and to advise courts about the suitability of the services in individual cases.

The Role of Social Workers

The policy has accelerated the development of dedicated social work criminal justice services and at the same time has promoted a change in social work practice. Although, in consequence, some criminal justice social workers have felt deskilled in relation to other areas of social work, dedicated services have arguably enhanced the skills of social workers in dealing with offenders. Social work criminal justice practice should have a primary focus on the responsibility of offenders for their behaviour. This contrasts with a focus on meeting the needs of offenders, the "welfare" approach which, until the Standards, had been characteristic of social work with offenders in Scotland since the Social Work (Scotland) Act 1968.

The attempt in National Standards to shift the primary focus from a welfare to a responsibility model of practice was echoed by MCG interviewees when commenting on the role for social work with offenders in the future. They saw it as no longer involving casework by individual social workers, but, rather, service provision by agencies with individual social workers accessing services which contribute to packages which will be effective in addressing offending behaviour.

Planning

To ensure that local resources and skills are directed towards meeting the objectives, priorities and Standards set out in national policy, a planning process was established. Planning was also intended to assist social work managers and practitioners by providing impetus and direction to service development, a basis for local consultation and a means of measuring performance and outcomes[25]. The first national planning statement was prepared jointly by The Scottish Office Social Work Services Group (SWSG) and the Convention Of Scottish Local Authorities (COSLA) in 1991. National Planning Statements are now produced on an annual basis and are subject to discussion in draft by the Main Consultation Group. At a local level authorities are responsible for the preparation, implementation and review of a comprehensive local annual plan and for the production of a three year strategic overview[26].

All interviewees were agreed that the planning process had many advantages, most notably, in the development of a more disciplined and consistent approach to planning and in engineering a greater sense of ownership of service and policy objectives amongst practitioners. Everyone agreed that planning had increased the range and quality and had enhanced the credibility of services.

On the other hand interviewees said that the effectiveness of this process and the implementation of the policy had been limited by the delay in developing national information systems and by the unavoidable uncertainty about whether the proposals in submitted annual plans would receive financial support. Local authority interviewees were concerned that the method of allocating funds might become too closely tied to workload measures. They pointed out that, for example, a decrease in the number of probation orders serviced by an authority might not necessarily imply a decrease in resource requirements as the use of probation for higher tariff offenders meant an increase in the resources required per probation order.

It was recognised that there was a balance to be struck between allocating additional resources to service innovation, redressing imbalance between authorities and the enhancement of under-developed services, such as throughcare. Nevertheless, the hope was expressed that the introduction of new planning arrangements for local government re-organisation in 1996 would lead to a better balance.

LOCAL CONTEXT

The commitment of the key professional groups to partnership was reflected at local level in the courts as well as in social work departments. Although local liaison arrangements were thought not to have changed

---

25 The planning system was reviewed and new National Standards and procedures introduced in 1994 to reflect planning experience to date. Further guidance was issued in April 1995 on the interim arrangements for planning subsequent to local government reorganisation and in March 1996 for the first year of the new councils.

26 Strategic Plans covering the period 1991-4 (and later years for Wallace and Bruce); Planning Statements covering the period 1993-95 (except Wallace which related to 1992-93).

significantly as a result of the policy, most criminal justice and social work interviewees at both national and local levels thought that liaison with the courts had improved.

National Standards had served to legitimise and formalise the process by requiring local authorities to develop effective liaison mechanisms. This creates an expectation that formal liaison would occur on at least an annual basis. Local liaison was characterised by both formal and informal meetings and generally was considered by social work managers and sheriffs to be effective. However, the opportunity to communicate effectively with sentencers in court was lessened if there was a high number of visiting sheriffs. Further, some sheriffs said that they would like more information about the outcomes of community disposals for high risk offenders.

The balance to be struck here is a very fine one - between ensuring the necessary communication with the judiciary and retaining the distinctive professional contribution which social work has to offer. For example, during interviews with social work managers the possibility was raised that court social workers in smaller courts might be perceived by sentencers as employees of the court rather than of the local authority. This meant that they would be less able to represent the social work department effectively. The potential for this was most notable in Bruce, a rural area, which had the smallest study court with a use of custody which was below the national average. In this court there was very close local liaison with the judiciary and this appeared to affect the capacity of social work to target services in a way which was consistent with National Standards. Though one of the main aims of the policy is to target probation on those most at risk of custody, as we show in Chapter Three, social workers in Bruce were less likely than social workers in the other study areas to target probation on high risk offenders.

The primary focus for liaison with the prison service was the production and review of social work unit management plans. Formal arrangements for liaison between local authority social work departments and prisons located within their geographical boundaries were believed by most managers to be reasonably satisfactory. However, in interview managers said that formal mechanisms for cross-authority liaison had not been established because of logistical difficulties.

Interviewees stressed that the organisational arrangements for the delivery of social work criminal justice services must be viewed in light of other social work services and, in particular, major developments in relation to the implementation of community care policy. Work with children and families was thought by several managers to have suffered most from the implementation of criminal justice and community care policies.

None of the authorities had established explicit guidance on determining which dedicated area should have responsibility for offenders requiring services which straddled different specialisms. Instead, there was an expectation in each authority that statutory work with offenders would be undertaken by dedicated criminal justice staff unless there were good practice reasons for doing otherwise. Such decisions tended to be made on an individual basis with individual welfare as the primary criterion for determining who should assume responsibility for the work.

CONCLUSION

Effective policy implementation requires good inter-agency communication and working. Government acknowledgement of this is reflected in the consultation and liaison arrangements which were central to informing the development of the policy. The main forum for national consultation, the Main Consultation Group, has been effective in promoting communication with the courts. However, interviewees said that the infrequency of meetings and nature of representation in the Group did not encourage the development of a strategic overview of policy implementation. Representation of criminal justice on the MCG has primarily reflected the prominence given to court focused services in the early stages of policy implementation. Policy implementation had been enhanced by the creation of arrangements for dedicated social work criminal justice service delivery. The planning process had contributed to policy implementation by clarifying objectives and priorities and locating service development within the context of national and local policy. Planning was believed to have enhanced the range and quality of social work criminal justice services.

At a local level, relationships between sentencers and social workers and liaison with the independent sector were thought to be good. Liaison with prisons tended to occur within individual authorities. However, cross-authority liaison with prisons and routine monitoring of prison social work was less satisfactory, perhaps reflecting the priority which has been given to non-court services during the early stages of policy implementation.

CHAPTER THREE
SOCIAL WORK SERVICES TO THE COURTS

INTRODUCTION

In this chapter we explore the impact of the policy on social work services to the court and sentencers' perceptions of its effectiveness. We consider the contribution of social work to reducing the risk of custody by analysing social enquiry reports (SERs). SERs are the means through which social work provides information about individual offenders and about the availability of services in the community. They help to shape criminal justice understandings: of offenders, of the potential for particular services and programmes to affect offender behaviour, and of social work's contribution to this process. We look at the contribution of social work to reducing the risk of re-offending by examining probation, a social work service which focuses on offenders addressing their problem behaviour.

Unless otherwise indicated this chapter draws on the findings of the study of sentencer decision making (Brown and Levy, 1998) and the probation study (McIvor and Barry, 1998). A full account of the methods used in these studies is provided in the study reports.

SENTENCER DECISION MAKING AND THE RISK OF CUSTODY

In order to understand the potential of social work intervention to impact on the risk of custody we need to appreciate the nature of sentencing. In both the study of early arrangements (McAra, 1998) and the study of sentencer decisions (Brown and Levy, 1998) sentencers were asked about their sentencing practice. The following discussion is based on the accounts which they gave.

Sentencer Decision Making

While the judiciary is constitutionally independent, sentencers exercise their discretion to interpret the law within the parameters set by statute and case law and by the High Court on appeal. Sentencers describe themselves as treating each case on its merits. They weigh and interpret information about the individual offender in the circumstances of the case, the offence, and the consequences of that sentence. To understand sentencing therefore we need to consider factors relating to the offender, the offence, the services which provide the detail of a disposal and how they are linked to produce a particular outcome[27].

---

[27] This is consistent with other studies of sentencing. See, for example, Rumgay, J. (1995), 'Custodial Decision Making in a Magistrates' Court', *British Journal of Criminology*, 35, 2: 201-217; Hogarth, J. (l971), *Sentencing: A Human Process*. Toronto: University of Toronto Press.

In relation to the offender, sentencers say they consider: the role that the offender played in the crime (for example, whether they were ringleaders or their involvement was peripheral); criminal history; the offender's response to previous sentences; the age of the offender; whether they had been at liberty or in custody during the current case; whether there are medical/psychiatric problems, or problems of substance misuse; the personal and financial circumstances of the offender. In relation to the offence, they consider: the nature of the crime; its seriousness, including factors which mitigate or aggravate crime; its significance (for example, whether there had been a spate of similar crimes in a locality); the harm to the victim; the public risk posed by the crime; and the public reaction to the crime. These factors are assessed in the context of an understanding of criminal behaviour as being the responsibility of individuals who are culpable because they have choice.

Sentencing Objectives

Sentencing is aimed at removing or limiting risk to the public and risk of re-offending. The sentencers interviewed said that they adhere to a range of objectives - to reform, restore, punish, denounce, contain, deter[28] - in order to achieve these broad aims and they emphasised the need to distinguish risk of re-offending and risk to the public. As one sentencer remarked

"...it's the sheriff who has to make up his mind not the social worker. It's not their job to balance the general interest of the public...against that of the accused. We have to take into account the fear and disenchantment of the public and to protect the public."

The policy is, however, concerned with only some of the sentencing objectives noted above and is focused on the risks of re-offending and custody. It is primarily based on a reformative and rehabilitative model of criminal justice, though there is a reparative element in community service. This sets limits to the potential for social work to impact on sentencing.

Social Work Influence

In order to assess the influence of social work services on sentencing practice, court statistics were analysed and interviews were conducted with sheriffs and in the four study areas. Criminal justice statistics indicate that since the introduction of the policy in 1991 there has been a slight increase in the use of custodial sentences by sheriff courts - from

---

[28] For a discussion of sentencing philosophy see Bottoms, A, (1995), The Philosophy and Politics of Punishment and Sentencing' *The Politics of Sentencing Reform* C.M.V. Clarkson and R. Morgan. Oxford: Clarendon Press. *The Report of the Interdepartmental Committee on the Business of the Criminal Courts* (Streatfield Report) points out that these objectives may be competing. See Curran, J. H. and Chambers G. A. (1982) *Social Enquiry Reports in Scotland*, Edinburgh; HMSO: 30.

11 per cent of all sheriff court sentences in 1991 to 15 per cent in 1994. In relation to young offenders under 21, a target group for the policy, the use of custody increased over the period from 14 per cent to 18 per cent. The use of probation for this group also increased from eight per cent in 1991 to 11 per cent in 1994 and is set in the context of a slight increase in the use of probation overall. More generally, there has been little change in the level of use of community service and a reduction in the use of fines from 67 per cent in 1990 to 61 per cent in 1994. The policy particularly aimed to reduce the use made of short custodial sentences and the direction of change in sentencing trends here is more consistent with the policy objectives. In 1991 61 per cent of custodial sentences from sheriff courts were for three months or less, whereas by 1994 the proportion had dropped to 53 per cent.

Sentencing statistics are affected by a range of factors: the level, types and seriousness of crimes, by changes in procedures (such as the extent to which it is decided to divert cases from the criminal justice system), as well as by judicial responses to the policy to improve the social work services provided to the criminal justice system. Together with the fact that social work services are only relevant to a small proportion of sentences given by the courts, these factors mean that sentencing statistics on their own cannot provide a clear indication of the impact of the policy.

In interview, sheriffs were asked about the factors which might affect their decision in those instances where an offender was borderline for particular disposals. In general, they said that they would consider community disposals where information indicated that there was a reasonable chance that it might prevent further offending; and where they had confidence that disposals would be thoroughly administered and supervised, with strict enforcement of breach. Factors identified by sheriffs as influencing the use of specific disposals are outlined in Table 3.1.

Table 3.1: Factors Influencing Sentencing Decisions

Disposal	Factors Influencing Decision
Custody:	Gravity of offence - where it is considered to indicate that custody is in the public interest, or that it will protect the public; As a last resort; When there has been disregard for an order of the court; If there is a high incidence of a particular type of offence within the locality; Where an offender lacks a stable residence and there is no supported accommodation available;
Community Service:	For serious offences where offender's problems have not been, or are not capable of being resolved through probation; Where an offender could benefit from disciplined work offering reparation to community;
Probation:	Where an SER has identified a problem which could be addressed through probation and if the offender is willing to co-operate; Availability of programmes, specialist group work, and intensive probation; Where offending is less serious;
Deferred Sentence:	Mainly for those requiring drugs or alcohol counselling but who do not require the additional support of probation supervision.

Thus, a range of factors was mentioned as affecting choice of sentence and, importantly, social work services can impact on some, but not all, of these[29]. It can impact on sentencing by providing: information about offenders and their circumstances; an assessment of their risk of re-offending and services which can impact on these; or unpaid work in the community as a penalty in place of custody. The Social Enquiry Report (SER) is the means for providing the court with information about these elements in relation to individual offenders and in some situations a court is required by law to obtain an SER[30].

SOCIAL ENQUIRY REPORTS

Following the 1968 Social Work (Scotland) Act a study of SERs in

---

[29] Social workers were more positive than sheriffs about the potential for probation to affect the behaviour of older recidivists. In Wallace social work department policy was to define sex offenders as being unsuitable for community service and, if they denied responsibility for the offence, as being unsuitable for probation. More detailed information is provided in Brown and Levy, 1998.

[30] National Standards 1991, Part Two paragraphs 1-2.

Scotland was undertaken in the late 1970s to examine the impact of the move from the former probation service[31] to generic social work services. Many of the issues identified in that study as being associated with resistance to the shift from specialist probation to generic social work practice, such as concerns about the quality and level of service in relation to social enquiry reports and probation, were present at the time of the introduction of the National Standards. These issues were intended to be addressed by the Standards.

Prior to National Standards, disagreement about whether SERs should simply describe, or whether they should make a professional assessment of, the circumstances of an offender, could lead to complaints that SERs were pleas in mitigation[32]. The wide discretion which at that time was given to social workers in relation both to the content and presentation of reports contributed to this difficulty. Few social work authorities had a formal policy on services to the court, and official and professional guidance on content focused on describing what reports should contain rather than explaining why the information might be relevant.

This situation has now changed and National Standards on SERs offer a structure within which social workers can present information to the court, together with an underpinning explanation of what information is required and why. Essential contents[33] for reports are specified and the Standards state explicitly that information should not simply be described but that its significance in understanding the behaviour of the offender should be explained.

The Links Between Policy and Practice

A well written social enquiry report was identified in the study of early arrangements (McAra, 1998) as one of the three factors which sheriffs said increased their confidence in the services provided for a given disposal[34]. Most interviewees at that time had commented that there had

---

[31] Curran, J. H. and Chambers, G.A. (1982) examined in detail a sample of 180 SERs from two social work authorities, conducted a survey of the social workers who prepared the reports and interviewed sheriffs about their experience of social work services to the courts and the impact of this on their willingness to use probation.

[32] This type of comment is still occasionally made today. For example Rumgay (1995) points out that much of the information with which social workers are concerned is also the concern of the defence agent when making a plea in mitigation. This implies that **how** social workers present their information can be as important as the information which is presented.

[33] Essential contents include: information relevant to offending (circumstances surrounding offence; offending history; attitude to offence; and personal and social circumstances contributing to offending behaviour); information relevant to disposal (response to previous disposals; financial information; family and employment responsibilities; physical and mental health; resources in community available to assist/supervise offender); review and conclusions; and recommendations. Full detail is provided at Part Two of the National Standards paragraphs 88-96.

[34] Others were feedback on the process and outcome of supervision, and guaranteed funding for services.

been major improvements in recent years in social enquiry report writing, especially in respect of the recommendations and conclusions. Interviewees agreed that National Standards had contributed to this although other factors mentioned were improvements in social work training and shifts in attitude on the part of some social workers. Where dissatisfaction was expressed it was because reports contained unnecessary detail or recommendations were thought by sheriffs to be unrealistic.

These findings were supported in the study of sentencer decision making (Brown and Levy, 1998) although in the later study, sheriffs said that reports had been "sharpened up" and noted improvements such as the inclusion of an action plan and assessment of offenders' attitudes to the offence, which they saw as enhancing the already high Standards of SERs. Though sheriffs said that absence of an action plan would not necessarily discourage them from imposing a probation order, they indicated that its presence could increase the likelihood of probation. Problems, or poor reports, were seen as being the exception rather than the rule and were attributed to organisational arrangements which generated conflicting demands and did not allow for adequate cover when staff were unavailable; social workers from other areas or non-specialist social workers preparing reports; and delays in accessing other agencies, especially health agencies.

Social Work Recommendations

In order to assess social work's impact on sentencing, social workers were interviewed about the preparation of SERs and a sample of SERs[35] from the four study courts was examined. Sentencers were interviewed about the influence of social work on their decisions. Sheriffs and social workers expressed broad agreement about the criteria for the use of different community disposals and most of the social work recommendations (65%) in the sample of SERs were accepted[36]. There was no difference in the level of missing information between reports where recommendations

---

[35] The sample was selected on the basis of social work recommendations for community service (20), probation (20), deferred sentence with social work services (10), and no recommendation (10). Difficulties in obtaining reports recommending deferred sentence with social work services meant that a sample of 212 reports was achieved. For fuller methodological information see Brown, L. and Levy, L. (1998).

[36] The proportion of sample recommendations accepted were 77% in Scott; 73% in Bruce; 62% in Burns and 42% in Wallace. The Sentencer Decision Making study used a quota sample therefore percentages do not indicate a rate at which recommendations in SERs in the study areas matched disposals. However, some studies have looked at this, for example, the Curran, J.H. and Chambers, G. A. study found that sentencers followed the recommendation in 69% of the reports in their sample with a recommendation. In a survey of social enquiry reports in Inner London in the 1980's the rate was 63% (Stanley, S. and Murphy, S. (1984), *Inner London Probation Service : Survey of Social Enquiry Reports.* London: Inner London Probation Service. See Gelsthorpe, L. and Raynor, P. (1995) 'Quality and Effectiveness in Probation Officers' Reports to Sentencers', *British Journal of Criminology*, 35, 2: 188-200. Returns to SWSG using the National Core Data System during the period from which the SER sample was drawn found overall rates of 41% for Scott; 33% for Wallace; and 58% for Burns. Figures for Bruce are unavailable.

were accepted and those where they were not. Sheriffs said that they tended to follow probation recommendations unless these failed to take account of the gravity of the offence. Variation across the areas was associated with differences between the offenders who were the subjects of reports in the study areas. In Wallace, a large urban court, where offenders had more previous convictions and were more likely to have previous custodial sentences, only 42 per cent of reports in the sample had recommendations accepted. In contrast, over 70 per cent of sample reports in Scott, also a large urban court, and Bruce, a small rural court, had recommendations accepted.

This underlines that, though well-evidenced and argued reports are likely to be more influential, the level of conversion of a social work recommendation into a sentence of the court should not be taken as an indicator of the quality of SERs. The type of offender targeted for services is an important factor. Further, conversion of a recommendation into a sentence is likely, at least in part, to be associated with other factors, such as those which sentencers indicated they consider when sentencing. Thus to use the level of conversion as a performance indicator in planning statements is problematic.

National Standards and the Content of SERs

The National Standards specify a range of topics which it is essential to include in social enquiry reports. These fall into four categories: information relevant to offending; information relevant to disposal; review and conclusions; recommendations[37]. The sample reports, chosen on the basis of recommendation, were analysed to identify the extent to which they included information relevant to offending and to disposal, and review and conclusions. To operate to the Standards social workers must do more than simply describe the information required for the categories. They need to offer an analysis of risk of re-offending, grounded in an explanation of an individual's choice to offend, which should be linked to a sentencing recommendation.

The **information relevant to offending**[38] which was most likely to be missing from sample reports was that about attitude to the offence - between 51 per cent and 71 per cent of reports across the four areas contained this information; and circumstances contributing to offending behaviour - which was mentioned in between 40 per cent and 68 per cent of reports. The **information relevant to disposal**[39] which was most likely to be missing from reports, was that about response to previous disposals

---

[37] See footnote 25 for a list of contents of these categories.
[38] Information relevant to offending covers: circumstances surrounding the offending; offending history; attitude to offence; personal and social circumstances contributing to offending.
[39] Information relevant to disposal covers: the offender's response to previous disposals; financial information; family and employment responsibilities; physical and mental health; community resources available to assist and supervise the offender.

- between 54 per cent and 69 per cent of reports across the four areas contained this information; and mental health - which was mentioned in between 20 per cent and 50 per cent of reports.

The **review and conclusions** generally had information about the feasibility of community disposals (in only 4 per cent of reports overall was this missing). However, fewer than half of reports contained other key information in this section. There was least information about:

- risk of re-offending - provided in between two per cent and 27 per cent of reports;
- the consequences of disposals for offenders and their families provided in between 16 per cent and 44 per cent of reports;
- offenders' views about the seriousness of the offence - provided in between four per cent and 20 per cent of reports;
- offenders' motivation to change - provided in between 27 per cent and 40 per cent of reports.

Advice To Sentencers

Despite the gaps in National Standards' information which was found in sample reports, in interview sheriffs said they were happy with the quality of the SERs which they received. Consistent with National Standards, social workers thought that the information on which they should focus was offending behaviour and they were clear about the importance of identifying the offender's attitude to the offence.

Table 3.2: Percentage of Sample SERs Providing Key Information

Key Information Required as Identified Mainly by Sheriffs	% age of Reports Providing Information
Family background/social history	96%
Employment	91%
Key Information Required as Identified by Sheriffs and Social Workers	
Pattern of offending	22%
Reasons for offending	62%
Prevention of further offending by appropriate community disposal	16%
Key Information Required as Identified Mainly by Social Workers	
Attitude to offence	67%
Range of appropriate disposals and conclusions	97%

Table 3.2 shows that the views of sheriffs and social workers about key information which should be included in SERs overlapped but did not match. Clearly there is a consensus about the importance of information on offending, although the provision of such information in SERs is very patchy. Even where such information was provided it tended to be descriptive rather than analytical. This meant that the potential for reports to assess the risk of re-offending was limited. The tendency to describe rather than analyse information was acknowledged by social workers in interview.

In contrast, a high proportion of reports contained information about family and employment, which is characteristic of a welfare approach. It is particularly noteworthy that sheriffs but not social workers identified this welfare type of information as key. Sheriffs viewed a good SER as one which contained information about the offence, the offender's attitude to the offence and their social and personal circumstances. They indicated that they particularly valued the information which SERs could provide about offenders' family and personal background, since they saw this as providing an indication of the cause of offending. This may be why sheriffs were content with SERs even though information was missing on other topics. When they seek an SER sheriffs already have an expertise in the individual criminal behaviour at issue. What they lack is information about the social and individual circumstances of the offender. SERs provide descriptive information about these circumstances.

Information on Offending

Though social workers had acknowledged the importance of the information listed in the Standards, they still provided the information characteristic of reports prior to the Standards and were less likely to provide analysis of how the elements of this contributed to offending behaviour, which is required in the Standards.

However, social workers generally had very limited information about an offence - often only the statement of charges (complaint) presented to the court, together with the offender's own version. Policy implementation in this respect appears to have been partial since effective arrangements for social work to have access to police reports and full criminal histories were not in place at the time of the research. The offender's attitude to the offence is much more easily obtainable and this together with social and personal circumstances was generally well presented in SERs. The lack of verified information about the offence presented difficulty for social workers in assessing offenders' suitability for particular disposals and consequently in making recommendations. Poor information on the offence can lead to inappropriate social work recommendations and unrealistic reports, a problem which was commented on by sheriffs and social workers alike.

Assessment of Risk

To operate within the Standards social workers need to concern themselves with the risks identified in the key policy objectives: risk of custody which directs social workers to targeting, and risk of re-offending which directs them to assessment and classification. However, we should note that although sheriffs said that when risk of re-offending is discussed this is generally helpful, they had mixed views about how far it was appropriate for social workers to be producing an assessment of this risk. Some sheriffs thought that such an assessment was difficult for social workers as the offender could "pull the wool over the eyes of the social worker" and that the sheriff was in a better position to make the assessment of risk of re-offending. This is a statement both about a lack of access to reliable information and about a lack of expertise in assessing the information. There is therefore a difference of understanding about what social work can say about re-offending. While the new social work approach within the policy has been broadly accepted in principle, the practical consequences of policy implementation have not been accepted by all.

SERVICING COURT DISPOSALS: PROBATION

We noted earlier that an important objective of the policy has been to provide credible services to sentencers, who would therefore be encouraged to make more use of them, since the services would address the problem attitudes and behaviour of offenders and lead to a reduction in re-offending. Although national statistics cited earlier showed a reduction in the use of short custodial sentences, sheriffs said that they were not aware of having changed their use of probation since the implementation of the policy. However, they said that improved reports and assessments had enhanced the credibility of social work services both for probation and SERs. In particular, the willingness of social workers to indicate when probation would not be a suitable disposal, had strengthened the credibility of recommendations for some sheriffs. Action plans could increase confidence in probation as could the availability of specialist schemes for drugs and alcohol counselling.

Probation aims to extend community based options to the court where the current and previous pattern of offending means that offenders are at risk of custody either immediately or in the foreseeable future. In order to look at the impact of the policy on the way in which court disposals are serviced by social work, the delivery of probation services and their impact on the short term risk of re-offending was looked at in each of the study areas.

National Standards For Probation

National Standards set out a framework within which social work services can give content to court disposals. The concern of the policy and of sheriffs is that probation should have the capacity to affect offenders' behaviour. National Standards state that probation should require offenders to work towards acknowledgement of responsibility for their behaviour and seek to reduce the risk of re-offending through a combination of supervision and control with help, encouragement and challenge. Probation should normally only be recommended where both control and assistance are needed and offenders have indicated that they are motivated to use probation to address their offending.

National Standards indicate that an SER recommending probation should always contain an action plan and in the probation study all but three of the SERs examined in case files contained such a plan. The plan identifies the objectives which the action outlined is intended to achieve. It should be agreed with an offender, presented in the SER and should state what will be done during the probation order to address issues associated with offending, together with the resources which will be used. The action plan therefore should convey a set of expectations about social work both to the court and to the offender. The plan is binding on the offender and failure to comply can result in formal action for breach. Additional requirements, such as attending a facility for psychiatric treatment, undertaking community service (known as section 7 orders), or attending an intensive probation programme, can be attached to probation orders.

Interviews with sheriffs in the initial phase of this research programme found that, with a few exceptions, sheriffs were generally satisfied with the provision of probation services. While National Standards were thought to have had a major impact in some localities, in others they were seen as having speeded up change already in progress. Greater information was now available to sheriffs about services and the range and quality of programmes were believed to have improved.

Sheriffs interviewed during the second phase of the programme held similar views and were generally satisfied with probation services. They emphasised that they attached importance to specialist schemes and to having information about the detail of probation and feedback on progress, especially where high risk offenders had been given a community disposal. Social workers and sheriffs said that prior to the Standards some offenders on probation were rarely if ever seen by their social workers. While National Standards had made probation a priority, some sheriffs still felt uncertain about what had happened in the course of probation orders and thought that completion reports did not say enough about whether the order had done any good in preventing further offending.

Offenders on Probation

A study of probation was undertaken by an examination of all 155 probation cases closed between July 1994 and April 1995 in the study authorities and, for a subsample of 112 of these probationers, social work case files were examined[40]. In addition questionnaires were completed by social workers in relation to 96 of these probationers and 65 probationers from this group were interviewed. A poor response rate in offenders allowing access to their files at Burns means that discussion of individual areas is restricted to Scott, Wallace and Bruce. When the characteristics of probationers in each area were compared, there was little difference found between the study areas in the gravity of offences for which probation was given[41].

Table 3.3: Characteristics of Probation Sample

	Percentage of Sample				Average Number	
	Women	Under 21	With No Previous Convictions	Who Successfully Completed Their Probation Order	Previous Convictions	Custodial Sentences
Wallace	16	51	12	50	10.0	2.3
Scott	14	50	14	76	7.6	1.4
Bruce	31	42	19	95	3.8	0.3

However, as table 3.3 shows, findings about other characteristics, such as criminal history, indicate that of the three areas, Wallace social workers were working with the most serious offenders, with offenders in the Bruce sample having much less serious criminal histories. Consistent with this, authors of the SERs for the probation sample in Bruce were least likely to think that offenders there were at risk of custody - 59 per cent were not thought to be at risk of custody, compared with 31 per cent in Scott and 38 per cent in Wallace. However, Bruce social workers were more likely to recommend additional requirements for probation orders - in 47 per cent of cases, compared with 20 per cent in Scott and 37 per cent in Wallace.

Targeting of probation on those offenders which National Standards state should be a priority was therefore least effective in Bruce, the small rural court. This had implications for the successful completion of probation

---

[40] For a fuller description of the methods and results see McIvor, G. and Barry, M. (1998) *Social Work and Criminal Justice: Probation.*

[41] The sample of offenders, 82% of whom were men, had usually been involved in summary cases heard at sheriff court (85%), often involving charges for dishonesty (57%) or assault/breach of the peace (19%), and had generally been placed on probation for 12 months or less (69%). The gravity rating used by Creamer et al (1992) *The Probation Alternative - A Study of the Impact of Four Enhanced Probation Schemes on Sentencing.* This assigns offences a rating of one to five, with the least serious offences being rated as one and the most serious being rated as five. For fuller details see McIvor, G. and Barry, M. (1998) *Social Work and Criminal Justice: Early Arrangements.*

orders. Overall, cases in which social workers thought that the offender was at risk of custody were three times as likely to be breached as those cases where custody was thought unlikely (47 per cent compared to 15 per cent). In Bruce, 95 per cent of probation orders were successfully completed, compared with 76 per cent in Scott and only 50 per cent in Wallace. Therefore, the lower rates of successful completion in Wallace and Scott were associated with the more effective targeting of the high custody risk offenders towards which the policy is directed.

The social work manager in Bruce indicated that the local sheriff was opposed to explicit targeting and to the inclusion in SERs of references to an offender's risk of custody. Unlike their colleagues in Scott and Wallace, social workers in Bruce did not use a formal risk of custody scale to assist them in targeting. They resisted the use of such scales since they saw them as undermining professional judgement.

As we shall see, the nature of targeting in an area, together with the response of social workers to the approach promoted in the Standards, impacted on the work which they undertook with offenders on probation. We consider this as we look at the use of the National Standards' framework for probation orders and examine the extent to which there was evidence of the responsibility model operating in the content of the orders and the role of social workers in probation.

Framework for Probation

The National Standards set a framework for operating probation orders which includes early implementation of the order; maintaining regular contact between the probationer and their supervising officer, as well as having a formal review of progress. A probationer must be seen by their designated supervisor not later than one week after the order is made. They should be seen weekly in the first month and fortnightly in the second and third months, with two of these appointments taking place in the offender's home. After this, appointments should be at least at monthly intervals.

Table 3.4: Percentage of Cases for which National Standards Were Achieved

	Wallace	Scott	Bruce
Initial meeting with supervising officer within 1 week	73%	69%	50%
Minimum of 8 contacts in first 3 months	52%	63%	5%
Timing of initial progress reviews within 14 weeks	67%	44%	37%

Findings confirm that, in the study areas, if there was ever a period when probationers had no contact with their supervising officer, this was now firmly in the past. However, the requirements for at least eight contacts in the first three months were met in only 44 per cent of cases overall in the study. Nevertheless, regular contact was maintained in all areas, with the average contact being around 13 visits for a 12 month order. Case notes in social work files indicated that where National Standards were not met this tended to be because the offenders failed to keep appointments or were unable to attend as they were on remand for other matters. Difficulties with travel in a rural area contributed to the low proportion of offenders in Bruce being seen within the period stipulated in the Standards.

Reviews allow assessment of the progress which has been made towards meeting the targets set out in the action plan. They also enable tasks to be identified for the next period of supervision. Bruce was least likely to conduct initial reviews within the three month period specified in the Standards. Difficulties in arranging reviews in a rural area may have contributed to this but, as we noted, management in Bruce identified that social workers there were resistant to National Standards in general and reviews in particular.

Wallace, the area with more young offenders considered at high risk of custody, had a high proportion (40 per cent) of cases with no reviews recorded on the case files (compared with 5 per cent in Bruce and 8 per cent in Scott). The lower number of reviews in Wallace appears to be accounted for by the higher level of non-compliance there - in that area more formal warnings were issued and more offenders were returned to court for failure to comply.

Action Plans

We explained earlier that the Standards have been based on the results of research on effective practice with offenders. They promote a change in social work understanding of offending and adjustment of practice. The SERs for the sample of probationers were examined to identify the explanations for offending, the action planned and the type of work undertaken on probation. Overall, the main explanations for offending given by social workers were related to alcohol use (34 per cent), drug use (21 per cent); opportunism (21 per cent); financial gain (19 per cent) and peer group pressure (17 per cent). Offending was most likely to be linked to alcohol and drug misuse in Scott[42] and financial gain in Wallace[43]. Offenders in Bruce were more likely to have their offending explained as a reaction to emotional pressures[44].

Similarly, in action plans although there was explicit reference to addressing offending behaviour in 73 per cent of cases overall, it was less

[42] Respectively 50% and 33% of cases; compared with 30% and 24% in Wallace; and 28% and 8% in Bruce.
[43] 31% compared with 13% in Scott and 10% in Bruce.
[44] 30% compared with 13% in Scott and 10% in Wallace.

likely to be mentioned in Bruce (35 per cent of plans) compared with Scott (78 per cent) and Wallace (82 per cent). Consistent with the findings about the explanations for offending, most action plans in Bruce (70 per cent) tended to identify relationships as an area to be addressed (compared with 38 per cent in Scott and 48 per cent in Wallace) and medical or mental health issues (30 per cent compared with 5 per cent in Scott and 6 per cent in Wallace). The research found evidence that probation practice was being adjusted according to the characteristics of offenders and their perceived needs associated with offending. In effect, this implies that the absence of targeting in Bruce was contributing to the focus on areas associated with relationships.

Action plans were rarely produced as separate documents in their own right and one consequence of this was that, though most probation cases had an action plan, most offenders said they were not aware of the existence of the plans. Nevertheless, most probationers said that they had discussed offending in some detail during their probation order.

Content of Probation

Overall, evidence about probation in Wallace and Scott was more consistent with the model of social work practice promoted by National Standards than was evidenced from Bruce, where findings were consistent with the continuation of a welfare model of practice.

There was little evidence of social workers in any of the areas operating as case managers (see Chapter Two) as most social work intervention took place on an individual basis and was carried out by supervising social workers themselves rather than through the use of specialist services. Analysis of case files indicated that if other agencies became involved in a case they usually assumed sole responsibility for providing the particular service concerned. Where other agencies were involved this was usually in relation to employment, alcohol, drug or health issues. Rural areas face particular difficulties in accessing services because of the uneven level of demand.

In most cases work was undertaken solely on an individual basis. Groupwork took place in relation to offending, employment, alcohol, drugs, leisure, physical/mental health and "other"[45]. However, groupwork was not a major activity as around 90 per cent of interventions on these subjects took place on an individual basis. Offenders who had attended probation groups or intensive probation programmes generally found such approaches to be stimulating and challenging.

---

[45] Other areas of intervention were undertaken solely by the supervising social worker. These were: relationships, financial accommodation, social skills, violence.

Short Term Outcome of Probation - Risk of Re-offending

At this stage in the research it has only been possible to look at the short term effectiveness of probation in impacting on offending. Overall, objectives related to changing the attitudes which supported offending, the provision of general practical support and improving the probationer's self esteem were most likely to have been achieved totally or to a significant extent.

Social workers and probationers had a shared view that probation had had an impact upon the risk of re-offending. Around three-quarters of probationers overall considered that they were less likely to re-offend than they had been prior to probation and social workers concurred. While around 70 per cent of probationers said they were unlikely to re-offend at all, social workers were less optimistic and thought that in practice this would be the case for around 40 per cent overall. Young offenders were thought more likely than adults to present a high risk of continued offending. Probationers were assessed as very likely to re-offend if their attitudes were unchanged, they had continued to offend while on probation; or they were entrenched in a pattern of offending behaviour.

For probation to be effective, probationers and social workers alike stressed the importance of being motivated to change and avoid offending, as well as being willing to contribute to the process. Three-quarters of probationers indicated that they had been motivated to address their problems when placed on probation, although younger offenders were less likely than adults to be motivated in this respect. Being highly motivated to address offending was associated with offenders being highly motivated to address other problem areas in their lives. The desire to avoid offending and its likely consequences or a wish to obtain help with other problems were thought by both social workers and probationers to be essential to a positive response to probation. There was agreement that features of probation supervision, such as the help received (including liaison with other agencies and advocacy), the relationship established with the social worker or the structure provided by the order, contributed to probationers' positive responses.

The relationship established with the social worker appeared to be a significant feature of the order. More than two-fifths of probationers indicated that a poor relationship with their social workers would have adversely affected their response to the order.[46] Given the importance of motivation in offenders making good progress, it was notable that most probationers were unaware that they could request a change of social worker. Only in one instance did a change result from a 'personality clash' between probationer and supervisor. However, in a few instances

---

[46] Palmer 1995 has highlighted the importance of the relationship with the supervising officer in effective working with offenders. Palmer, T. (1995) 'Programmatic and Non-programmatic Aspects of Successful Intervention: New Directions for Research' *Crime and Delinquency* 41, 1:100-131.

probationers indicated that they had tried to get their supervisor changed but that their views had been ignored.

CONCLUSION

The results of this research show that the policy on social work services to the courts has made a substantial impact on a number of important aspects of social work services. The policy has had a positive effect on the judiciary's view of social work services. Sentencers now express greater confidence that community disposals will be thoroughly administered and supervised and this was largely borne out by the research on probation. Sentencers were satisfied with the Standards to which SERs were generally written and the major effort which has been made in relation to liaison with the judiciary has helped to promote understanding of what social work can provide.

However, on a number of key issues there is a need for further progress. Inadequate access to verified information about the offence limited the potential for assessing risk of re-offending. Even where this information was presented in a report, it was not always linked with information on the personal and social circumstances of offenders, to provide a basis for assessing risk of re-offending. This affected the credibility of proposals for services which could contribute to reducing that risk. The National Standards require clear links to be made between individual offending and social circumstances. The research did not find that these links were being made. SERs tended to describe rather than analyse information about offenders and often did not make the required links explicit.

The probation study found that overall, probation practice was being re-focused on addressing offending. Two of the study areas were targeting higher risk offenders and were working more consistently to National Standards than the third area. In this area targeting of services did not reflect the policy priorities and there was evidence that the approach of social work was more consistent with the welfare model of practice and less consistent with the approach which the Standards are promoting.

The principal target group for this policy - young offenders at high risk of custody - posed particular difficulties for probation. Younger offenders were less likely to have been motivated to address offending and other problems, were slightly less likely to have demonstrated some reduction in risk of re-offending, and were much more likely than adults to have been breached. The study area with the highest proportion of young offenders at high risk of custody, was also most likely to have negative outcomes to probation. This indicates that, to the extent that there is effective targeting of offenders at whom the policy is directed, a higher level of breach needs to be anticipated. More generally, it illustrates the importance of setting service outcome indicators which are appropriate for particular groups of offenders. However, there is an absence of information on patterns of recidivism at national level. This makes it difficult for local authorities to set outcome targets against re-offending rates.

Some elements of the Standards, such as the action plan, were not always being fully used. Research on effective work with offenders has identified the need for clear expectations to be communicated to offenders. Action plans are a means through which this can be achieved, but offenders were not always aware of their existence and what they contained.

Though the policy has encouraged the development of dedicated criminal justice social work services, specialisation by individual social workers supervising offenders on probation was less apparent and most social workers were providing a broad range of services. There is scope for further development of specialist resources and, particularly in rural areas, for the development of models of service delivery which will take account of the variable levels of demand.

CHAPTER FOUR

SOCIAL WORK, PAROLE AND THROUGHCARE

INTRODUCTION

Social work provides services in relation to custodial as well as community based disposals. In this chapter we consider how the implementation of the policy has impacted on social work services to the Parole Board and how this has affected decisions about the appropriate timing of release for prisoners. We explore social work effectiveness at the throughcare stage through considering services which have been developed for prisoners and their families to help with resettlement in the community and the avoidance of reoffending on their release. This chapter draws on research reported in McAra 1998a and McIvor and Barry, 1998a.

We have noted that an important part of the policy is about communicating the contribution of social work to others. However, in contrast to the position of the judiciary as members of the MCG, the Parole Board which is responsible for advising about the release and recall of prisoners on licence, was not represented on the MCG at the time of the research[47]. To some extent this indicates the priority which was given to throughcare in the early stages of implementation. As we shall see, lack of communication is a feature of a number of problems which this research programme has identified with policy implementation in relation to throughcare.

In Chapter One we pointed out that risk to the public was notably absent as a distinct risk addressed by the main policy objectives and was underdeveloped within the National Standards. It is in the section of the Standards which deals with throughcare that the few references to public safety occur. However, these are only in passing, except in relation to offenders against children and sex offenders. Even here, risk to the public is neither systematically nor explicitly integrated into the detail of the Standards (see footnote 18). We consider this as we look at how the Standards have affected social work's impact on the Parole Board and offenders.

---

[47] MCG membership includes Scottish Office administrators with responsibility for criminal justice, social work and parole matters. There was Parole Board representation on some MCG sub-groups.

THE PAROLE BOARD

The Parole Board for Scotland[48] advises on the release of prisoners on licence or on recall from licence, the conditions of licences and the variation of these conditions. The Board therefore considers applications for the release of prisoners with determinate sentences, those with indeterminate (that is, life) sentences, and for the recall of people on parole or life licensees.

When examining a case the Parole Board can consider the prisoner's social and criminal history before their current sentence; their work record and domestic background; the circumstances of the current offence; and the prisoner's response to any intervention and training during current sentence. The Board takes into account a number of questions about the prisoner when reaching a decision. These are whether the person is at risk of committing a further serious offence; whether they have co-operated with training in prison and made best use of prison facilities; whether they have progressed sufficiently to a stage where further imprisonment would be unlikely to impact on their prospects of leading a useful life on release; and whether they have personal support in the community and suitable accommodation[49]. As with sentencing, social work can impact on only some of the factors which the Board consider important. The study found that, when considering cases, the Parole Board were operating with an explanation of criminal behaviour based on a model of individual responsibility.

The basis of the Board's decision is the information contained in the dossier it receives for each case. The dossier contains prison staff reports, a prison social work report and a home circumstances report prepared by the social work department in the area to which the prisoner is to return. It may also contain other documents, such as a psychiatric or psychological report, or a letter confirming an offer of employment. A police report and a note on the circumstances of the offence prepared from Crown Office papers (note of circumstance) may be added to the dossier when it is presented to the Board. When making a decision the Board looks at the range of documents in the dossier and the extent to which they confirm or disagree with each other. While the prison social work report is an important source of information about risk, the Board also considers the prisoner's own account of the offence, as outlined in their representations, together with the official account provided in the note of circumstance or the police report. In assessing release plans the

---

[48] The membership of the Board must include a judge, a psychiatrist, someone with knowledge or experience of the supervision or aftercare of discharged prisoners, and someone who has studied the causes of delinquency or the treatment of offenders. For a detailed description of the statutory basis of membership of the Board and of parole see McAra, L. (1998a) *Social Work and Criminal Justice: Parole Board Decision Making*. Since 1996 the Parole Board decides on parole release and recalls cases where the sentence served is under 10 years.

[49] Parole Board Annual Reports quoted in McAra, L. (1998a).

Board looks to both the prison social work report and the home circumstances report. The effectiveness of services provided in prisons, the quality of information provided in the reports, and the range and quality of services which are provided in the community affect Parole Board decisions. Social work reports therefore constitute elements of a range of material which is assessed by the Parole Board in individual cases.

IMPACT ON THE PAROLE BOARD

The initial implementation study (McAra 1998) found that Parole Board members who were interviewed thought that the quality of some reports had improved, but that the quality of reports was variable and dependant on the experience and ability of individual social workers. Interviewees said that community-based social work services were generally improving although there was greater scope for inter-agency working. At that time the guidance in *Continuity Through Co-operation*[50] was thought to have enhanced co-operation between different service providers in a number of prison units. However, Parole Board members thought they had insufficient information about available services in the community and commented that better liaison with social work, both at the level of policy and at the level of service delivery, could address this. Findings at Phase Two have shown little change with the exception of evidence that early views about the impact of *Continuity Through Co-operation* appear to have been over-optimistic.

A more detailed study was undertaken in the second phase of the research programme[51]. The study found little evidence that social work information and services within the community were making a substantial impact on Parole Board decisions. In interview, Parole Board members said that they did not think that the policy had encouraged them to release more prisoners early. Observation of Parole Board decisions in 253 cases for which there was the potential for a recommendation for provisional release, identified that in only 15 per cent (39) were factors relating to social work services given as a contributing reason for the decisions that were made. Cases where social work had this type of impact on Parole Board decisions were more likely to involve sex offenders; to be at their second or subsequent review; and to have only a short period remaining available for parole.

---

[50] *Continuity Through Cooperation* SPS/SWSG February 1990.

[51] The study involved observation of all six Parole Board meetings which were held between January and March 1994; detailed analysis of all cases considered at the meetings; analysis of a sample of 68 prison social work reports and 63 home circumstances reports drawn from the parole dossiers of cases considered at the meetings for each of four prison units; semi-structured interviews with four members of the Parole Board for Scotland; four prison social workers; and a group interview conducted with community based social workers from each study site. Details of this study and its findings are presented in McAra, L. (1998a). New throughcare standards were issued in March 1997.

In order to explore this limited impact of social work on the Parole Board we shall consider prison social work reports and home circumstances reports.

Information to the Parole Board

Social work reports should provide the Parole Board with an assessment of the prisoner's experience of imprisonment, an assessment of the circumstances into which they will be released, together with the likely impact of each of these on the potential for re-offending. Community based throughcare services are intended to assist with the reintegration of prisoners into the community and social work reports to the Parole Board are expected to outline the services which will be available should an individual prisoner be released.

Prison Social Work Reports

National Standards say that prison social work reports should be based on two interviews with the prisoner and liaison with the social worker who will carry out the supervision in the community. Most prison social workers interviewed said that since implementation of the Standards they always made contact with the social work department in the area to which the prisoner would be returning. Although this generally worked well, there could occasionally be problems caused by delays in appointing a supervising officer for a case. However, not all interviewees thought this contact was necessary and, in fact, most reports analysed for the study were identified as having been based on only one or two interviews with the prisoner (69 per cent) with no mention being made of contact with the community social worker.

Not all social workers were sympathetic to the Standards. In particular, prison social workers were less positive and, in interview, questioned whether they should be providing the range of information outlined in the Standards. However, community social workers who deal with fewer throughcare cases welcomed the structure of the Standards.

National Standards require eleven types of information about the prisoner's personal circumstances to be indicated and assessed within prison social work reports. These are shown in Table 4.1 which indicates that, overall, the reports examined for the research tended to **indicate** rather than **assess** information.

Table 4.1: Prison Social Work Reports: Information Provided and Assessments Made

Type of Information	% Provided*	% Assessed*
Personal Circumstances	100	72
Response to Imprisonment	94	66
Attitude Towards the Offence	90	59
Employment Prospects/Use of Leisure	87	51
Family/Other Significant Relationships	85	50
Substance Misuse/Gambling Problems	82	46
Response to Previous Supervision	53	46
Risk of Re-Offending	51	34
Services Available in the Community	50	26
Attitude Towards Sentence	38	24
Attitude Towards Release Plans	12	10

*N = 68

No reports in the sample covered all types of information and three reports made no assessments at all. As with SERs, prison social work reports were more likely to provide information consistent with a "welfare" model of social work. Information which the "responsibility" model requires was much less likely to be provided.

Parole Board interviewees recognised that the quality of reports was very uneven. They saw the main purpose of the prison social work report as being to provide information on the extent to which the prisoner was demonstrating responsibility through their plans for release, progress in custody and the extent to which significant problems associated with offending had been addressed. Key information which the Parole Board sought, and which is consistent with the Standards, relates to the potential for reoffending and often, as the table shows, this was not provided. Observation of Parole Board meetings confirmed that prison social work reports were an important source of information about risk of re-offending and the extent to which an offender had addressed their problem behaviour. This underlines the difficulty posed by the high levels of omissions about risk of re-offending and attitude to release plans.

Prison social workers indicated that assessments were easier to make for those prisoners who had had prior contact with social work services. Information on which to base assessments was sometimes patchy and its accuracy could depend on the quality of information provided by area social work teams or the quality of the prisoner's own account, as workloads meant that there was little opportunity to verify information. Social workers said that it was their practice to seek agreement from prisoners before accessing records about their response to previous supervision. When dealing with prisoners who had no previous social work contact[52] or who would not agree that the social workers should access their records, social workers found assessments were particularly difficult to make.

In relation to risk of re-offending, social workers said that they did not generally have access to verified information about the offence or about previous convictions and that they often had to rely on prisoner accounts. Therefore the information necessary to provide the re-offending risk assessment sought in the Standards was not always available.

Home Circumstance Reports

Observation of the Parole Board indicated that home circumstance reports were generally used as a basis on which to comment on the level of family support, and this information was found to be well covered in the home circumstance reports analysed. In other respects, findings on home circumstance reports broadly mirrored the problems identified with prison social work reports. Community based social workers provide the report on a prisoner's home circumstances, which covers the supervision and support which could be provided to the prisoner on release, and contributes to the assessment of risk of re-offending or social breakdown by the prisoner. National Standards say that home circumstance reports should be based on at least one visit and interview with the offender's family, and contact and liaison with the prison social worker. In interview social workers said they always made contact with the prison social worker, though they acknowledged that this could be difficult if the prison social worker was in a singleton post. Nevertheless, only 19 per cent of reports gave information that indicated that they had met the standard for liaison with prison social workers. Most (65 per cent) indicated that they were based on one interview with the family, and a few reports (16 per cent) gave no indication that there had been contact with either the prison social worker or the family.

National Standards require six types of information about the prisoner's personal circumstances to be **described** and **assessed** in these reports, which should contain a release plan for meeting the prisoner's needs.

---

[52] Scottish Prison Service policy is that prisoners should not be seen as people in need of treatment but as responsible people who can choose to make use of services during their sentence. (*Opportunity and Responsibility*, Scottish Prison Service (1990): HMSO).

Table 4.2: Home Circumstances Reports: Information Provided and Assessments Made

Type of Information	% Provided*	%Assessed*
Background (family, housing, financial)	94	76
Family attitudes to prisoner	90	38
Environment to which prisoner will return	75	46
Specialist resources and programmes in the community	48	46
Family's likely response to social work supervision of prisoner	43	10
Assessment of support		73
Assessment of risk		40
Assessment of need		32

*N = 63 Percentages add to more than 100 as reports included more than one type of information

Table 4.2 shows that, as with prison social work reports, home circumstance reports tended to describe rather than assess information. Fifteen per cent of reports in the sample described all six types of information and 15 per cent of reports made no assessments at all. Only 15 per cent of reports provided an assessment of the three elements of support, risk and need. Of the 40 per cent of reports in the sample which included an assessment of risk, most focused on the level of family support which the prisoner would have on release.

The Prison - Community Social Work Link

The concept of throughcare implies co-ordination between prison and community social work services. Thus the release plans in both prison social work and home circumstance reports should be complementary and should be aimed at minimising re-offending risks and assisting the prisoner to reintegrate into the community.

Just under half of prison social work and home circumstance reports had a release plan. There was a particular reluctance to develop release plans for prisoners who were seen as being high risk and therefore unlikely to get parole. Most prison social workers interviewed thought that the release plan was the responsibility of the community based social worker who would have better information on the suitability and availability of community resources. However, community social workers thought that it was the province of the prison social worker to provide this package because they would know the prisoner better and be in a better position to assess needs[53]. Community social workers generally said that a proper assessment of risk of re-offending could only be undertaken if the social worker had direct contact with the prisoner. It was not always possible for community social workers to travel the sometimes lengthy distance to prison to see individual prisoners and, in one study area, managers would not provide the resources for such visits, even though they are covered by 100 per cent funding.

PAROLE BOARD DECISIONS AND RISK

We emphasised earlier that the policy is primarily focused on risk of custody and of re-offending. Of these, only the second was identified by the Parole Board as being of concern. Board members said that risk of re-offending and risk to the public, understood as danger, were important in the decisions which they made. Risk of re-offending was their prime consideration, except when looking at the possibility of recalling people on parole or life licences, when danger was an explicit concern of equal importance to re-offending. Observation of Parole Board meetings identified that when there was discussion of social work services it tended to focus on the potential for rehabilitation within prison and the potential for supervision and control within the community.

Prominence of Risk in Decisions

Risk of re-offending had least prominence in considerations of indeterminate (i.e. life-sentence) cases. This was because the original crime had often been an isolated incident. The Board focused on sustained progress in custody, as indicated by good behaviour; taking advantage of facilities; addressing significant problems (e.g. addiction); and a positive response to testing in open conditions, such as on home leaves, or on work placement in the community. There was little discussion of release plans and family support, or mention of services identified by social workers to assist in reintegration into the community. In these cases, therefore, the potential for prison social work impact would appear to be greater than that of community social work.

A focus on risk of re-offending was more prominent in determinate cases and there was a consensus amongst Parole Board members about indicators of risk. These were: nature and circumstances of the current offence; number and pattern of previous convictions; extent to which the offender had accepted responsibility for the offence and had addressed

---

[53] The new Throughcare Standards state that: "Social workers in prisons must try to engage the prisoner in the development of a realistic and achievable release planning." (para 105). Although the social worker in the community should also prepare a release plan including the availability of specialist resources, standards did not state that he/she should interview the prisoner. The social worker in prison must, however, liaise with the social worker in the community to review the provisional plan after notification of the release date.

their offending behaviour together with any associated problems such as substance misuse; the level of support the offender would have on release; plans for managing time in the community, for example, employment. Levels of risk are therefore assessed on the basis of information about past behaviour, change in custody and future structures. Clearly social work services have the potential to impact on some of these indicators, for example, change in custody, through addressing offending or addictions, and elements of future structures, such as the structuring of the ex-prisoner's time. Other aspects, such as past behaviour, are not amenable to social work impact.

Level of Risk

Cases assessed as low risk were released. They were seen as having good release plans with supportive relationships, having addressed offending and associated problems, having few previous convictions or a good response to previous social work. Cases considered by the Board to be high risk often had more than one adverse indicator present and were not usually recommended for release.

> "No matter how good the release package they're not likely to get parole if the level of risk hasn't changed..." (Parole Board Member)

Where high risk cases were recommended for parole this was generally because they were nearing the end of their sentence and therefore had only a short period of time available for parole. In these circumstances the Board wished the prisoner to experience social work supervision on release, as this supervision was held to be a form of control. However, Parole Board interviewees indicated that their discretion to use short periods of parole to control offenders is likely to reduce in the future[54].

Nature of Risk

It was when considering the group of cases for possible recall that the Board explicitly distinguished between risk of re-offending and risk to the public. Offenders were recalled because they had committed (or were charged with) further offences, or because they had breached other conditions of licence. High risk offenders in this group were thought to be those with serious offences/charges involving violence, and those with a history of similar convictions. In these cases the focus for discussion and the determining factor was the danger to the public posed by the offender. Whereas the Board must be alerted when someone has been convicted of an offence, at the time of the research, social workers had

---

[54] Changes introduced in the Prisoners and Criminal Proceedings (Scotland) Act 1993 extend the use of supervision in the community. For those sentenced after 1 October 1993, instead of simply being released at the two-thirds point of their sentence, prisoners serving four years or more who do not get parole will be released on licence for the remaining third of their sentence.

some discretion in relation to charges[55]. However, the policy's lack of a clear distinction between risk to the public and risk of re-offending meant that there was an absence of guidance about the circumstances under which social workers should advise the Board about charges which ex-prisoners may be facing but which have not been to proof.

Impact of the Policy on Social Work and Parole

Some Parole Board members wanted more feedback about the success of parole and social workers wanted to be told about the outcomes of Parole Board decisions. At the time of the research, Parole Board members thought that end of parole reports were inadequate. As we have seen, reports were not consistently providing the information set out in the Standards. In particular, information about offending, a key element in using the Standards, was not always based on verified evidence. The extent to which prison and community social work were communicating about individual prisoners was unclear. Although social work reports were not found to have made a substantial impact on Parole Board decisions, the important information which the Parole Board was seeking, for example about risk of re-offending and the availability and suitability of specialist resources, was often absent. The full potential for social work to impact on Parole Board decisions can only be tested when reports containing the information set out in the Standards are provided to the Board.

THROUGHCARE SERVICES

A key aspect of throughcare is statutory supervision. The primary objectives of statutory supervision, as set out in the National Standards, are to assist offenders to reduce the risk of re-offending, to help with resettlement in the community, to ensure compliance with licence conditions, and to facilitate early release of prisoners eligible for statutory supervision[56]. Services are required by the Standards to focus on these objectives. Interviewees in the study of early arrangements believed that throughcare was the least well developed social work criminal justice service prior to policy implementation and therefore had the most progress to make. At Phase Two there appeared to have been a little progress but much remained to be done.

The research programme examined throughcare services in the study areas in order to consider the impact of the Standards on the

---

[55] New throughcare standards have removed this discretion:
"The supervising officer must notify SOHD immediately he/she becomes aware that a licensee has been charged with a further offence during the period of supervision of the licence. There is no discretion in this matter." (paragraph 232).
[56] National Standards Part 2: Throughcare paragraph 8.

effectiveness of throughcare services[57]. The research on throughcare involved an examination of all 60 throughcare cases in the study authorities (parole, statutory and voluntary aftercare) which closed between July 1994 and April 1995 and where prisoners had been released from custody since April 1992 (when National Standards came into effect), including life licensees released at that time. We look at the use of the National Standards' framework for the throughcare of this group and consider the extent to which there was evidence of the approach promoted by the Standards being operated in the content of throughcare services.

Ex-Prisoners Receiving Throughcare

Most of the sample were male and over 20 years old, with life licensees being older on average than other groups. Around half were imprisoned for non-sexual crimes of violence and one in four for drugs offences. The average length of a determinate sentence was 40 months. Most parole licences were for periods up to 12 months, and just over half of parolees had additional requirements attached to their licences by the Parole Board, usually involving drug or alcohol counselling, residence at supported accommodation and treatment for sex offending. There was little difference in the sample across areas in the gravity of offences.

Framework for Throughcare: Prior To Release

Effective throughcare requires good communication and liaison between agencies. National Standards state that, for prisoners who will be subject to parole or statutory aftercare on release[58], one month prior to the release date the prison social worker should convene a meeting with the prisoner and the social worker responsible for community based throughcare to refine plans, agree the allocation of tasks and set out expectations for the first three months of release[59]. Evidence of this was patchy, with only around half the sample showing evidence that the pre-release contact outlined in the Standards had actually been made. It is possible that some contacts were unrecorded on file, but in some instances the distance of the prison from home or the limited time available between parole being granted and the date of release had precluded the three way meeting set out in the Standards from taking

---

[57] Information on the 60 cases was collected from social work files and questionnaires were completed by social workers in relation to 48 of these and 31 of this group were interviewed. The majority of the sample (41) were parolees, including seven life licensees. Others had been provided with voluntary assistance, had been subject to statutory aftercare or, in one case, had been subject to a supervised release order. In three of the study areas the sample was drawn from across the authority, while in the fourth it was drawn from two area teams. Burns, where only five ex-prisoners agreed to access, was too small for reliable separate conclusions to be drawn about throughcare in that area.

[58] For a detailed description of the distinction between statutory supervision and voluntary support see McIvor, G. and Barry, M. (1998a).

[59] National Standards, (1991), para 55.

place. Only about a third of ex-prisoners interviewed recalled this meeting taking place, and in only one instance did an ex-prisoner indicate that prior to their release there had been a written agreement about issues to be addressed during parole.

Although some ex-prisoners interviewed identified examples of constructive help they had received from prison based social workers, most thought that prison social work had been unhelpful, and that the procedure for requesting services was obstructive. Prison social workers were seen as being uninterested, unless people were lifers or sex-offenders; not trustworthy with confidential information; and unwilling to provide a service for those who did not accept their guilt.

Framework for Throughcare: After Release

The Standards indicate that on release there should be early contact with the supervising social worker, regular contact after that and formal monitoring of progress. Most ex-prisoners (77 per cent) subject to statutory throughcare were seen within one working day of their release, the time scale stipulated in the National Standards. Those requesting voluntary assistance were first seen around six weeks after release.

Standards for contact between supervising social workers and ex-prisoners on statutory supervision were met for 52 per cent of the 46 in the sample for whom information was available.

The National Standards indicate that at the end of the first three months of supervision a formal review should be held which should involve the ex-prisoner, the supervising social worker, the social worker's first line manager, if appropriate, and other key people. Just over half of reviews (52 per cent) fell outside the period specified in the Standards.

The Content Of Throughcare

At the pre-release stage most services appeared to focus on practical matters such as employment, financial matters, accommodation, and offending. After release, relationships, financial matters and accommodation were prominent. With the exception of services relating to employment, offending and alcohol, most work was carried out directly by the supervising social worker on an individual basis. Of the 13 areas of service identified, only in relation to offending, employment and alcohol,[60] were post-release services provided on a group or a mixed basis. Nevertheless, group work was still a minor activity on these topics. Although other agencies provided services in relation to accommodation, finance, offending, employment, alcohol and health,

---

[60] The remaining areas were: accommodation, relationships, finance, drugs, use of leisure, education, violence, health, social skills, other.

48

services provided by other agencies constituted only a small proportion of the services delivered.

In most individual cases social workers and ex-prisoners were agreed about the main issues. Consistent with the Standards, avoiding or addressing offending was the issue most often identified as being significant by social workers. However, ex-prisoners gave more emphasis to accommodation and employment and thought that social workers underestimated the significance of accommodation and overestimated the importance of offending. Alcohol, family and personal relationships were also identified by social workers as prominent issues.

The research team asked social workers to identify objectives in each case and to say how far they thought they had been achieved. Overall 59 per cent of objectives were assessed as having been achieved in full or to a significant extent and in only six per cent of objectives was no progress thought to have been made at all. Table 4.3 indicates the type of objectives identified and percentage achieved overall; where numbers are small no firm conclusions can be drawn about a particular objective.

Table 4.3: Throughcare Objectives and Social Workers' Views about Their Achievement

Topic of Objective	Number of Cases	Percentage of Cases	Number Achieved	Percentage * Achieved
Offending	30	62	19	63
Employment/education	21	44	11	52
Accommodation	18	38	6	33
Re-settle in community	13	27	9	69
Alcohol	11	23	8	73
Family relationships	10	21	6	60
Personal relationships	8	17	4	50
Get through licence	8	17	7	88
Other practical issues**	8	17	6	75
Drug use	5	10	1	20
Emotional support	5	10	2	40
Other factors***	5	10	4	80

*Completely or to a significant extent

**Financial issues, practical support and use of leisure time

***Violence, peer group, other attitudes supportive of offending

Social workers indicated that re-settling in the community, avoiding further offending and help with family or personal relationships were the objectives most likely to have been achieved completely or to a significant extent. Financial objectives, those related to employment or education and those relating to accommodation were, on the other hand, most likely to have been achieved only partially, to a limited extent or not at all.

Most ex-prisoners were said by their social workers to have been motivated to address their offending and other problems, and three-quarters of the sample were thought by their social workers to have responded positively to throughcare. Features of the throughcare contact were seen as contributing to this - the help received, the relationship established with the social worker or the clear framework provided by a statutory order.

Though the effectiveness of throughcare was seen as being ultimately dependent on the motivation of the ex-prisoner, social workers recognised the importance of material improvements in ex-prisoners' lives. They were also aware that most ex-prisoners valued practical or general support and the opportunity to discuss their problems. The role of the social worker - the relationship established, the availability and responsiveness of the social worker and the social worker's objectivity - were also thought by social workers to be important. Ex-prisoners' responses to throughcare were described as poor in fewer than one in eight instances. Factors which had adversely affected their responses included social or personal problems which detracted from their ability or willingness to comply, reluctance to engage with the social worker, personal characteristics, and the influence of offending peers.

Offender Views

However, two-thirds of ex-prisoners interviewed had a more negative view of throughcare. They saw supervision as part of their prison sentence and a deterrent to re-offending but nevertheless still had expectations about social work support. Around half of interviewees recognised that avoiding further offending was an expectation of them while on licence and about a third mentioned the need to keep appointments with the social worker. Most saw parole as a reward for good behaviour within custody, some saw it as a chance to prove their worth on release and to be re-integrated into the community.

Most indicated that, prior to release, they had high expectations, hoping that throughcare would provide them with practical help with employment or education, accommodation and re-settling in the community. The research found though that some expectations were unrealistic and that ex-prisoners' disappointment undermined the credibility of the social worker. On termination of throughcare only about one in four ex-prisoners believed that their situation had improved as a direct result of social work services. The rest thought that their circumstances had not improved or, if they had, that they themselves had achieved the change on their own.

RISK OF RE-OFFENDING

The research found little evidence of deliberate non-compliance with supervision, with few in the sample being charged or convicted of further offences during their period of social work supervision following their release (19 per cent or 9 out of 48) and only two being re-called to prison. Those charged or convicted tended to have more previous convictions (11.7 compared with 5.6) and to be younger than others in the sample (21.8 years compared with 34.3 years).

Sixty-five per cent (30) in the sample were believed by their social workers to be unlikely to re-offend, 24 per cent (11) were thought fairly likely to re-offend and in the remaining five cases further offending was considered very likely. As in the probation study, offenders who were described as highly motivated to address their offending and other problems were least likely to be considered at risk of committing offences in future. Social workers thought that further offending was unlikely because: the original offence had been isolated, or because of the time which had elapsed since it occurred; there was offender motivation to avoid re-offending, including recognition of what they had to lose and insight into their behaviour and its consequences; there was stability in current circumstances; and improvement in the ex-prisoner's circumstances since the commission of the offence.

Risk of further offending in the future was seen as being indicated by continued offending during the throughcare period and by the existence of factors associated with offending, such as alcohol or drug misuse. For just under half of the sample the risk of re-offending was considered by social workers to be unchanged since their release from custody and just under half were thought to be less at risk following throughcare. In four cases (8 per cent) ex-prisoners were thought by social workers to be at greater risk of re-offending because of the removal of formal controls provided by statutory supervision. For 19 of the 21 cases where risk of re-offending was thought to have reduced (i.e. 40 per cent of the sample of 48), social workers thought throughcare had contributed to that reduction.

In almost two-thirds of cases where further offending was believed to be less likely at the end of throughcare supervision than when offenders were first released from prison, social workers thought that offenders' increased self awareness and understanding of the consequences of behaviour were key factors.

Offender Views

Interviews were conducted with 31 ex-prisoners and it was found that most thought it unlikely that they would re-offend. National Standards state that in helping ex-prisoners re-settle in the community social workers should help them:

"... to understand, recognise and tackle positively those aspects of attitude, behaviour and pressures which contributed to past offending and the most recent custodial sentence". (National Standards, 1991, para 72.1)

Eighty-one per cent (25) of the ex-prisoners interviewed believed that they were at less risk of re-offending than when they were first released from custody. However only nine considered that their social work contact had contributed to this reduction. Most thought that offending was an irrelevant issue frequently raised by the social worker and emphasised their own motivation to stop offending and the importance of their personal and social responsibilities.

CONCLUSION

Overall there was mixed evidence about the extent to which National Standards were being implemented in relation to the provision of information to the Parole Board and services for throughcare. This means that the impact of the policy on performance and outcome has not been fully tested.

Reports to the Parole Board were found to have had a minimal impact on decisions. Their impact may have been limited because of patchy information, especially in relation to the risk of re-offending and the tendency to describe rather than to assess the information provided. As with SERs, there were difficulties with access to verified information about the offence and this meant that reports were not necessarily being prepared on as reliable a basis as the Standards are promoting.

As a result of limited communication, Parole Board members, offenders and social workers had different understandings about the contribution of social work to throughcare. Thus the Parole Board looked to prison social work to address the risk of re-offending and understood that community based throughcare was providing supervision or was focusing on re-integration into the community. Ex-prisoners were seeking help with their social and other circumstances. Like the Parole Board, they thought that the issue of offending had been addressed by or within prison and that social work concerns about re-offending after release were irrelevant. However, consistent with the approach promoted in the Standards, community social workers focused on individual ex-prisoners' responsibility to address offending.

While there appeared to be liaison arrangements within particular social work departments and between local community and prison social workers, no arrangements were found to be in place for liaison with prison social workers in other local authorities. This limited communication about the preparation and content of reports. Prison and community social workers did not agree about who should take responsibility for developing release plans; one result of this was that fewer than half of the reports in the sample had release plans.

The Standards promote the use of a release plan in order to communicate clearly to the Parole Board and to ex-prisoners what the objectives of throughcare services will be and how they are to be met. However, most ex-prisoners were not aware of these plans. Further, the Standards for contacts with prisoners following release were met in only around half of the sample. For this reason the research found that the framework for throughcare set out in the Standards was less well used than was the framework for probation.

In relation to parole and throughcare, therefore, though there appears to have been some re-adjustment of social work practice, much more is required if the responsibility model embedded in the Standards is both to be implemented in practice and communicated to those outside of social work, whether Parole Board or offenders themselves.

CHAPTER FIVE
CONCLUSIONS

INTRODUCTION

In this chapter we consider what the findings from the research programme indicate about policy implementation and its impact on the contribution of social work to reducing the use of custody and the risk of re-offending. The policy is directed towards shaping professional social work understanding and practice and criminal justice expectations about the potential of social work to contribute to criminal justice.

We have characterised the change required within social work as involving a shift from a welfare model of practice, where individual welfare is the primary concern and offending a secondary issue, to a responsibility model, in which the main focus is on offending and welfare issues are of secondary consideration. As well as involving structural alterations in the organisation of social work criminal justice services, this involves a fundamental change in social work culture, that is, the routine understanding and practice of individual social workers. The organisational and management changes necessary for dedicated services in this sphere of social work have been set in place by policy and senior managers responsible for services. However, changes in professional social work culture, so that the responsibility model comes to be understood and broadly accepted as "good practice", take much longer to establish. It is important to recognise that, while the policy has moved beyond the initial stages of implementation, the research was undertaken at an early stage in making progress towards achieving the long term objectives of establishing social work services and practice which will be effective in reducing the risk of custody and the risk of re-offending. The final part of this research programme will look at outcomes for the sample of offenders studied in the main phase of the research.

PROGRESS TOWARDS PRINCIPAL POLICY OBJECTIVES

Use of Custody

The first of the principal policy objectives is concerned with reducing the use of custody:

> "..... by increasing the availability, improving the quality and targeting the use of community based court disposals and throughcare services on those most at risk of custody, especially young, adult repeat offenders".[61]

---

[61] Research Evaluation Strategy Paper, September 1990

There was mixed information about the impact of the policy on reducing the use of custody by the courts and reports to the Parole Board were found to have had a minimal impact on decisions about release of prisoners. The courts viewed the information provided in SERs as useful. The Parole Board were less positive about the information provided in prison social work and home circumstance reports, and important information, such as about release plans, was often missing. The impact of all social work reports was limited by difficulties which social workers had in getting access to reliable information about offending. Where information was available, social workers tended to use it descriptively rather than to assess its significance.

In general social workers were servicing probation orders efficiently and the courts had more confidence in making this disposal. Some areas were found to be successfully targeting services on young offenders at risk of custody. However, young offenders are less likely than adults to be highly motivated to address offending and other problems, less likely to have reduced their risk of re-offending and more likely to breach their probation orders.

Reducing Re-Offending

The second of the principal policy objectives is concerned with reducing re-offending:

> "to enable offenders to address their offending behaviour and make a successful adjustment to law-abiding life".[62]

There was evidence from the probation and the throughcare studies that both social workers and offenders thought that there had been some success in addressing the risk of re-offending, at least in the short term. Longer term follow up of the samples in these studies, which will be undertaken in the third and final phase of this research programme, will provide information on how far this success has been sustained.

PROGRESS TOWARDS THE INTERMEDIATE POLICY OBJECTIVES

The policy had a number of intermediate objectives which were set out in Chapter One. We shall briefly review how far these have been achieved before moving on to reflect on the overall impact of the policy.

Strengthening Community Based Disposals

Progress has been made in relation to two of the court focused intermediate objectives. These are concerned with strengthening community based disposals and improving their availability to the courts.

---

[62] Research Evaluation Strategy Paper, September 1990

The implementation of the National Standards and the priorities set for the provision of social work services were found to be making a substantial contribution here.

Although National Standards' timescales for certain activities, such as contact with probationers, were not always being achieved, the framework for probation provided in the Standards was generally being used. Within this framework, in two of the three areas for which it was possible to collect evidence, there was information that probation services were being effectively targeted towards offenders at risk of custody and that probation activity was directly focused on addressing offending. However, there was some evidence that the welfare model continued to pervade social work approaches to probation. This was particularly the case in the area which showed least evidence of targeting, which was least likely to meet National Standards' time-scales and where social workers were more likely to undertake work focused on relationships, use of leisure time and physical or mental health. Importantly, this was a rural area therefore some elements of the Standards, for example, timescales for contact with probationers, may have posed practical difficulties. Nevertheless, this was also an area where there was close liaison with the court and where there was evidence of resistance from social workers to the model of practice promoted within the Standards.

This illustrates a dilemma for social work: the policy promotes a particular understanding of good social work criminal justice practice. However, if courts in particular localities make it clear that they have a different view, should local social work adjust to that view, or should it, on the basis of a professional social work judgement of what constitutes appropriate and effective social work, sustain a distinctive professional approach? If the first view is accepted then this poses a problem for having National Standards at all. If the second is accepted, then, as the situation above illustrates, the professional change required by the Standards may, in some areas, be contested and therefore may take longer to be brought fully into effect.

Services to the Courts

The third court focused objective, concerning arrangements for effective liaison with the courts, has been substantially achieved. There was consistent evidence from the studies on the programme that the courts now have confidence in the quality and efficiency of social work services and that this confidence has increased, particularly in relation to probation.

Sentencers were generally satisfied with the quality of SERs. However analysis of reports indicated that they often did not provide an assessment of risk of re-offending, which is a key requirement of the Standards. Rather, the welfare model was still prominent in the type of information which social workers were providing in reports. There were structural reasons for this, in that social workers did not have access to verified information about the offence. But there was also evidence that even where the relevant information was presented in a report, it was not always used to provide a basis for assessing risk of re-offending. The responsibility model requires explicit links to be made between an offender's behaviour and their social circumstances. The research did not find that these links were being made.

Sentencers thought that reports were now more focused and valued the information which they provided, especially about offenders' attitudes to their offending. They were less convinced that assessment of risk of re-offending was the legitimate province of social work. This implies that, while the general direction of the policy has been accepted by sentencers, some of the detailed practical consequences which will flow from full implementation may receive, at least initially, a less enthusiastic response.

Services Following Custody

A further policy objective, relating to information to the Parole Board and the quality of throughcare, was to improve both the voluntary and the statutory supervision of released offenders in order to encourage earlier release on licence and compliance with licence requirements. Overall, there was mixed evidence about the extent to which National Standards were being implemented in relation to the provision of information to the Parole Board and services for throughcare. Throughcare had not been a particular priority within the implementation of the policy and least progress had been made in improving the quality of statutory or voluntary supervision for released prisoners. This means that the impact of the policy on social work performance and outcome in these services has not been fully tested.

Communication on Release

The information which Parole Board interviewees said they looked for in prison social work reports and home circumstance reports was broadly consistent with the Standards. However, as with SERs, information about risk of re-offending was not often given in reports and, where it was, reports tended to present the information without analysing it. The reasons for reports not meeting the Standards were both structural and professional/ cultural.

There were two structural problems. The first was associated with the policy in prisons of prisoners only making contact with social workers if they chose. The second was associated with the absence of effective mechanisms for social workers to access verified information about the offence. This meant that social workers had difficulty securing reliable information. Unless prisoners had opted to use social work services in prisons, social workers would have no contact with them prior to the preparation of the prison social work report. This, together with the lack of verified information about the offence, limited the potential for social workers to make assessments. However, professional resistances were also evident and, for example, social workers were unwilling to access information from social work records without prisoner agreement. Where this was not forthcoming, they were restricted in what they could provide in reports.

The research on parole and throughcare identified that communication needed to be improved between Parole Board members, community social workers and prison social workers. Members of the Parole Board did not think they were well-informed about social work policy, services or outcomes of parole supervision; and social workers wanted more feedback about the outcomes of parole considerations in particular cases.

While there appeared to be liaison arrangements between local community and prison social workers, no arrangements were found to be in place for liaison with prisons in other local authorities. This limited communication about the preparation and content of reports. One result of this lack of communication was that fewer than half of prison social work and home circumstance reports in the sample had release plans, as prison and community social workers did not agree about who should take responsibility for developing these. Yet release plans were specifically mentioned by Parole Board interviewees as contributing to their deliberations about release.

A more general consequence of restricted communication was a gap in understanding between Parole Board members and social workers about where the balance of social work practice should lie. Risk of re-offending was a problem which the Parole Board expected to be addressed in prison. Where this had not happened offenders were likely to be seen as high risk and would not usually be released. Community based throughcare was seen by the Board, not as addressing re-offending, but as providing supervision or as focusing on re-integration. However, National Standards require community social workers to attend to risk of re-offending.

Strengthening Throughcare

The study of throughcare found that, consistent with the Standards, social workers focused on individual responsibility to address offending. Ex-prisoners, however, were seeking help with their social and other circumstances. Like the Parole Board, ex-prisoners thought that the issue of offending had been addressed by or within prison and that social work concerns with this after release were irrelevant.

In relation to parole and throughcare, though there appears to have been some re-adjustment of social work practice, much more is required if the responsibility model is to be both implemented in practice and communicated to the Parole Board or offenders themselves. Evidence on effective practice with offenders stresses the importance of setting objectives, linking planned work to these and communicating this information clearly to offenders so that they can understand what is being proposed and why. Release plans offer one means of informing offenders about the objectives for throughcare and how these can be met, but the research found that their potential remained under-used.

Young Offenders

One policy objective was to develop services targeted at a specific group of offenders - young adult offenders at high risk of custody. Evidence on achievement here was mixed and there is scope for more development of specialist resources for this group. Young offenders posed particular difficulties for probation and the development of specific services was uneven across the study areas.

Findings in relation to young offenders highlight the difficulties with establishing meaningful performance indicators. Younger offenders were less likely to have been motivated to address offending and other problems, were slightly less likely to have demonstrated some reduction in risk of re-offending, and were much more likely than adults to have breached their order. This means that monitoring information relating to achievement of particular targets during the probation process, such as the number of reviews undertaken, and particular outcomes, such as level of breach, need to interpreted with care. The study area with the highest proportion of young offenders at high risk of custody, was also most likely to have probation orders breached. The area with the least effective targeting was found to have the highest proportion of successful short term outcomes. Therefore, to the extent that there is effective targeting of offenders at whom the policy is directed, a higher level of breach and more negative short term outcomes need to be anticipated.

More generally this illustrates the importance of setting service outcome indicators which are appropriate for particular groups of offenders. There are, however, difficulties for local authorities in setting these levels because of the absence of information on patterns of recidivism at national level.

Arrangements

Objectives related to the efficient and effective organisation, management, and delivery of services to the courts are largely in the process of being met[63]. The main forum for national consultation, the

---

[63] Monitoring has not been discussed in this report and therefore we have omitted a discussion of the research finding that this objective has not been successfully met. Full discussion is provided in the study by Brown, L. Levy, L. and McIvor, G. (1998) *Social Work and Criminal Justice: The National and Local Context.*

Main Consultation Group, set the tone for policy implementation. The composition of the MCG reflects the prominence which has, to date, been given to court-focused services. While the MCG has therefore been effective in promoting communication with the courts, communication with the Parole Board, which is not represented on the MCG, has been less effective.

At a local level relationships between sentencers, the independent sector and social workers were thought to be good. On the other hand, liaison with prison social workers, other than on a formal basis within individual authorities and routine monitoring of prison social work was less satisfactory.

CONCLUSION

Most of the major structural changes to organisation and management necessary to facilitate specialist criminal justice social work services have been set in place. In the longer term full implementation of the policy will require fundamental cultural changes within social work practice. Professional cultural changes, that is changes in the routine understanding and practice of individual social workers, so that the responsibility model comes to be understood and broadly accepted as "good practice", take much longer to establish.

The research found that some of the required structural changes had not yet happened: detailed links between social work and criminal justice agencies were not fully operational, for example, there were difficulties with social work access to verified information about offending. The significance of access to offending information not being in place is that it is only very recently, and associated with the new policy, that social workers have been expected to have anything to say directly about criminal behaviour in individual cases. The research found, however, that even where verified information was available, social workers did not always make use of it. Indeed, some social workers showed unwillingness to access individual social work records without prisoner agreement. More often than not, the information within social work reports was characteristic of the welfare rather than the offence focused responsibility model of social work practice.

This illustrates some of the structural and cultural features which inhibit full realisation of a key shift required by the policy - from social workers as experts in welfare to the production of a new kind of social work expertise - an expertise in risk assessment to assist with the targeting of organisational resources and to indicate their potential to impact on criminal behaviour. It is important to recognise that while the policy has moved beyond the initial stages of implementation, it is still at an early stage in making progress towards achieving the long term objectives of establishing criminal justice social work services and practice which will be effective in reducing the risk of custody, where appropriate, and the risk of re-offending. The policy is in the process of refocusing the contribution of social work in this area from a primary concern with the welfare of individual offenders to the requirements of criminal justice.

As others[64] have noted, sentencers and social workers share a common concern with offenders as individuals. Recent research conducted elsewhere has emphasised that, in addition, social work has a distinctive contribution to make:

> "..sentencers reading reports valued an individualised assessment of the circumstances, needs and potential of offenders, and this gave strong support to...a document informed by social work skills and values." (Raynor, P. Gelsthorpe, L. and Tisi, A. 1995: 483)

This programme of research has identified the distinctive contribution of social work as being concerned with individual and social responsibility which aims to minimise the situations in which criminal choices are more likely to be made. While the National Standards address both aspects of responsibility the relationship between these and the implications for social work practice require further clarification and development.

---

[64] Curran. J. H. and Chambers. G. A. (1982).

PART 2

SUMMARIES OF THE STUDIES

INTRODUCTION

The Policy

In Scotland, statutory social work services to offenders and their families are provided by the local authority social work departments. Since April 1991, the Scottish Office has reimbursed to social work departments the full costs of providing a range of statutory social work services in the criminal justice system. National Objectives and Standards (the National Standards) were introduced by the Social Work Services Group of the Scottish Office to coincide with the introduction of the 100 per cent funding initiative.

The National Standards and the 100 per cent funding initiative cover: social enquiry reports; court social work services; probation; community service; and community based throughcare (social work in prisons is funded by the Scottish Prison Service). Since 1991, the initiative has been extended to supervised release orders, bail information and accommodation schemes, and supervised attendance order schemes (the latter two schemes are not yet available on a national basis).

The main aims of the Government's policy are:

- to reduce the use of custody by increasing the availability, improving the quality and targeting the use of community-based court disposals and throughcare services on those most at risk of custody, especially young adult repeat offenders;

- to enable offenders to address their offending behaviour and make a successful adjustment to law-abiding life.

Background to the Research

Central Government's review and evaluation of implementation of the funding initiative and the National Standards involves a programme of inspection by Social Work Services Inspectorate (SWSI), interpretation of statistics and a programme of research. The research programme is being conducted in three phases and examines progress towards policy objectives.

The main purpose of the study in the first phase was to examine the responses of key criminal justice decision makers and Scottish Office officials to the principal objectives of the policy and the early arrangements for its implementation. The main aims of the second phase have been to assess policy implementation and the extent to which it has resulted in achievement of the policy objectives. The final phase of the research programme will focus on longer term outcomes.

Study Sites

Four sheriff court areas, each in separate social work authorities, were selected as study sites for the second phase of the research programme. The sites reflect areas of both high and low population density and represent both specialist and more generic forms of organising social work criminal justice services. The names of the four areas have been anonymised in reports and are referred to as Scott, Wallace, Burns and Bruce.

EARLY ARRANGEMENTS

INTRODUCTION

This is a preliminary study (Phase One) which examines the perceptions of key criminal justice decision makers and Scottish Office officials about the principal objectives of the policy and the early arrangements for its implementation. The findings are based on analysis of the National Objectives and Standards document and on interviews in 1992-1993 with 12 sheriffs (2 from each of 6 sheriffdoms); one procurator fiscal from each sheriffdom; two members of the Parole Board for Scotland; and four Scottish Office officials. Their views were obtained on the effectiveness of the implementation of the National Standards; facilitators and inhibitors of implementation; and the impact of early implementation arrangements on sentencers' willingness to make use of non-custodial disposals. The research was undertaken 19 months after the 100 per cent funding arrangements had been implemented.

KEY FINDINGS PART ONE

Implementation of the National Standards: Central Government Experience

The research has identified that there is a tension in the policy between the framework of the objectives and standards and the need to develop services within available resources. In fulfilling its tasks in social work services in the criminal justice system, key concerns of Central Government focused on strategic planning and the national core data system.

Strategic Planning

The social work professional view of strategic planning was that it had a key role to play in enhancing the performance and outcome of local authority services, whereas the administrative view was that it should be primarily finance focused. Variations in responsibility in relation to the policy may at least partly explain different official assessments of the adequacy of policy implementation. The professional view was that strategic planning had progressed well although local authorities required more time to develop planning skills and adequate management information systems. The administrative view however was that it had had limited impact so far and that many local authorities developed plans without sufficient consideration of the availability of Central Government money.

National Core Data System

The national core data system was seen as essential to the development of performance and outcome indicators which could help to assess service delivery. Interviewees identified a tension that had arisen between the funding of service delivery and the development of the monitoring system. Officials agreed that the national core data system had been slow to develop.

Implementation of the National Objectives and Standards: Sentencers' Experiences

Three factors were identified as increasing shrieval confidence in a disposal: feedback on the process and outcome of supervision, a well written social enquiry report and guaranteed funding for services. However increased confidence in disposals did not appear necessarily to guarantee that a particular disposal would be used more frequently and may have no part to play in decisions taken about serious categories of offence.

The research found a divergence between the aims of the National Objectives and Standards and the sentencing aims of sheriffs. Although sheriffs were willing to endorse the reformative and rehabilitative model of criminal justice which informs the standards, when sentencing offenders at high risk of custody, punishment rather than the nature or quality of social work input to community based disposals, was a major consideration. Sentencers believed that this was compatible with public interest. Sheriffs thought that shifts in sentencing practice away from custody in recent years had been precipitated by court of appeal decisions although they acknowledged that National Standards implementation had contributed to change.

Liaison

Co-operation within Central Government had worked well during the consultation phase of the policy and interviewees were concerned that this level of co-operation should be sustained. Sheriffs and procurators fiscal thought that National Standards implementation had had minimal impact on liaison arrangements and that these were already satisfactory, although procurators fiscal expressed concern about the effectiveness of liaison in cases where a child was the victim.

KEY FINDINGS PART TWO

Local Authority Implementation of Service Standards

Scottish Office officials agreed that the local authorities had been slow to implement the policy initially but that it was now being progressed much more quickly.

Three facilitators of policy implementation were identified: the protection of resources through the 100 per cent funding initiative, the development of specialist services integrated into service delivery systems as a whole and the National Objectives and Standards framework.

There were variations in view as to whether impediments to policy implementation had been organisational factors; differing priorities within Central Government; the policy context within which the policy was being implemented; or the nature of the 100 per cent funding arrangements.

Officials thought that the local authorities had been reluctant, in the early stages of policy implementation, to recognise the contribution that the independent sector could make to service provision. Factors in this were thought to be local authority fears about privatisation, the variable quality of independent sector provision and inexperience on the part of the local authorities in managing the purchaser/provider relationship.

Social Enquiry Reports

The majority of interviewees commented that there have been major improvements in recent years in social enquiry report writing, especially in respect of the recommendations and conclusions. Reports are generally delivered on time although they are often only available on the morning of the court. Interviewees agreed that National Objectives and Standards implementation had contributed to this although other factors mentioned were improvements in social work training (which were believed to have developed over the last ten years or so) and shifts in attitude on the part of some social workers. Where dissatisfaction was expressed it was because reports contained unnecessary detail and recommendations thought by sheriffs to be unrealistic.

Probation

Sheriffs were generally satisfied with the provision of probation services. National Objectives and Standards implementation was considered to have had a major impact in some areas. Greater information was now available about services and the range and quality of programmes was believed to have improved. Nevertheless sheriffs generally thought that there was further scope for development. In some areas improvements in services were not attributed to National Objectives and Standards implementation which was seen as having speeded up change already in progress.

Community Service Orders

Interviewees' perception was that the National Objectives and Standards for community service (which have been in place since 1989) had had minimal impact. Most sheriffs thought that community service had always been good in their locality. Others commented that it was poorly supervised and concerns were expressed about the resourcing of services in some areas. Assessments for community service were seen to be of higher quality when undertaken by specialist community service workers. Although some sheriffs wanted to see wider use of community service, others felt that this would undermine the credibility of community service as an alternative to custody and wanted to see the maximum number of hours increased.

Breach of Community Service/Probation Orders

In some areas procurators fiscal believed that social workers lacked knowledge about requirements for breach procedures. In areas where breach procedures worked well liaison was identified as contributing to this.

Services for Young Adult Offenders

National Objectives and Standards implementation was considered to have had minimal impact on the development of specialist schemes although a wide range of services was developed prior to implementation and this was continuing. Intensive probation was viewed favourably. However concerns were expressed that insufficient attention had been given to the development of schemes aimed at young people involved in less serious offences.

Throughcare

Throughcare was believed to be the least well developed social work criminal justice service prior to policy implementation and therefore had the most progress to make.

Reports

Though some interviewees thought that the quality of home circumstance reports and prison social work reports was variable and linked this to the experience and ability of individual social workers, others thought that the quality of reports had improved, reflecting more thorough input from social workers and increased co-operation between agencies.

Social Work Services in Prisons

The implementation of the guidance in *Continuity through Co-operation* was thought to have enhanced co-operation between different service providers in a number of prison units. Although in some areas increased levels of counselling had enhanced the effectiveness of prison-based social work, some interviewees thought the provision of this service was patchy and prisoners in some units lacked contact with social workers.

Community Based Social Work Services

Parole Board members thought they had insufficient information about available services and commented that better liaison with social work administrators could address this. Interviewees considered that community-based social work services were improving although there was greater scope for inter-agency collaboration. There were variations in view as to the extent to which the independent sector and local authorities should be involved in service provision.

The key findings of this report will be explored in detail at Phase Two of the evaluation which looks at the impact of the policy on the process and effectiveness of service provision.

The full report of the study is *Social Work and Criminal Justice Volume 2: Early Arrangements*, Lesley McAra, (1998).

THE NATIONAL AND LOCAL CONTEXT

INTRODUCTION

The purpose of this study is to describe the national and local context within which the policy was developed, implemented and reviewed prior to and during the period in which the research programme was conducted. Findings are based on an analysis of central and local government policy and planning documents, and interviews in spring 1995 with: five members of the Main Consultation Group on Social Work Services to the Criminal Justice System; twelve social work managers; and seven independent sector service providers.

Views obtained from representatives of the Main Consultation Group and Scottish Office documents provide an assessment of policy implementation at the national level, and local government documents and views of social work managers, court social workers and social workers provide a view of policy implementation at the local level. In some instances, the national view conflicted with the local view (in the study areas) and in other instances, policy implementation at the national level was seen to have inhibited or facilitated implementation at the local level. These issues are identified in the following discussion which summarises the findings in respect of: consultation; planning and funding; organisational structures; and monitoring.

CONSULTATION

National consultation, which is conducted primarily through the Main Consultation Group, was generally seen by those members interviewed to have been effective in involving key stakeholders in developing the National Standards and generating a sense of ownership of them.

The Judiciary

Some Main Consultation Group interviewees suggested that the Group could have approached the judiciary for more assistance in raising awareness of policy implementation and in the pursuit of a more coherent judicial response to the development of services. At the local level, interviews with sheriffs (Brown and Levy, 1998) and social work managers indicated that formal liaison with the judiciary did not always take place in all of the study areas and, where this existed, it was not always effective. Some sheriffs, however, were reluctant to participate in formal liaison but identified a need for more information on the performance of offenders and success of orders. Such information could be provided at formal liaison meetings (Brown and Levy, 1998). Informal liaison, in particular between sheriffs and court social workers, was viewed by them to be operating well.

Procurators Fiscal

Some Main Consultation Group respondents considered that the proposed inclusion of diversion within 100 per cent funding had given impetus to the development of links with procurators fiscal and to the development of more coherent systems for interacting with court agencies. Although managers reported that formal arrangements had been introduced in two areas, liaison was generally conducted on an informal level. Managers and those procurators fiscal who were interviewed considered that existing arrangements were satisfactory.

Prisons

At the national level, liaison between the Scottish Prison Service (SPS) and social work criminal justice services could, some Main Consultation Group representatives believed, be more effective. In addition they, and the findings of the inspection (SWSI, 1993), indicated that liaison between community based and prison based social workers could be improved. At the local level, whilst liaison between social work departments and prisons within their boundaries was seen to be satisfactory, managers considered that the absence of formal mechanisms for cross-boundary liaison could be compounded by the creation of a larger number of smaller authorities following local government reorganisation.

Independent Sector

At the national level, networks between local authorities and the independent sector could, some Main Consultation Group members believed, have been exploited to a greater extent. However, at the local level, social work managers and independent sector providers in the study areas considered that, in general, the nature and extent of liaison had been adequate. Nevertheless, they recognised that some factors had, where they existed, possibly prevented relationships from being more productive: the absence of service agreements; a lack of regular contact with social work teams to ensure a constant flow of referrals; staff turnover in the local authority; and the lack of a joint forum for joint discussion of strategic issues. However, the National Standards were considered by managers and independent sector providers as having facilitated good liaison arrangements which resulted in greater accountability.

PLANNING AND FUNDING

Planning

The strategic planning process was seen by managers to have engendered a greater sense of ownership of service and policy objectives amongst practitioners and to have disciplined authorities to conduct internal reviews consistent throughout Scotland. The planning process was believed by managers to have contributed positively to the development of services by providing a focus for the development of services and establishment of priorities within an overall objective.

Interviewees and documents reported that the preliminary planning procedures, introduced on a national level, did not operate effectively at the local level and that absence of reliable information systems at both the national and local levels hindered strategic planning. Steps have been taken to remedy these problems: revised planning procedures have been introduced and the system for providing national information has been reviewed.

Managers, sheriffs and social workers (Brown and Levy, 1998) identified a need for a wider range of specialist services and an increased quantity of available places. Interviewees reported that rural areas experienced particular difficulties in accessing or providing services. The absence of a sufficient number of places or an appropriate specialist service could, some sheriffs argued, dissuade them from imposing a non-custodial sentence in some cases. If the courts' needs for services are not met, this could inhibit the achievement of policy objectives.

Main Consultation Group respondents and managers believed that a more collaborative approach to providing and developing services would be required with smaller authorities following local government re-organisation as smaller authorities would be unable on their own to offer a comprehensive range of services because of diseconomies of scale. This, managers believed, might discourage the independent sector from providing services to smaller, predominantly rural, authorities. Sheriffs (Brown and Levy, 1998) were concerned that the full range of services might not be available which would limit the options in each case and the risk of custody might thus become greater.

Funding

Phase One of the research programme which was conducted in 1993 (McAra, 1998), identified a tension between the framework of the National Standards and the need to develop services within available resources. This tension was still apparent during the fieldwork of the present study. Managers and local authority plans expressed concern about obtaining an appropriate level of funding to develop existing services, establish additional specialist services and introduce more innovative methods of work. In general, managers highlighted the need to prioritise carefully to ensure that standards in the core areas of service delivery were met, which might be at the expense of introducing more innovative and potentially more effective methods of work.

Throughcare was considered by Main Consultation Group interviewees and managers to be an area that was still under-developed, despite local authority plans identifying this as an area of priority. Reasons for the slow progress in developing throughcare provided by managers and some Main Consultation Group interviewees included: the relative priority which prison management attributed to the service; the separate funding of social work in prisons; it is resource intensive on account of travel costs and staff time; and the relatively low number of offenders receiving throughcare services.

Managers and interviewees in the Phase One research (McAra, 1998) believed that availability of 100 per cent funding had protected core services. The absence of 100 per cent funding for diversion and services associated with monetary penalties had, managers believed, hindered development of a comprehensive approach to planning and service delivery. Managers suggested that the difficulty of managing smaller budgets might preclude the flexibility which currently existed in larger authorities to meet the costs of services not subject to 100 per cent funding.

ORGANISATIONAL STRUCTURES

A range of organisational structures had been adopted by the four study areas: from specialist offender services teams to teams in which social workers spent part of their time on other services (Scott), and from generic to specialist middle and senior management. The shift to greater specialisation and the introduction of the National Standards were viewed by managers, court social workers and some sheriffs, as having resulted in improvements in the preparation of SERs and probation. However, McIvor and Barry (1998) found that the National Standards were most closely met in the area whose teams were less specialised. On the other hand, managers considered that the areas in which the greatest progress had been made in introducing more structured offence focused methods of probation work, were those which had the clearest specialist structures. Brown and Levy (1998) found that the quality of SERs did not differ significantly between the study areas.

Some social work managers believed that there was a risk of returning to generic models of service delivery in rural authorities where pressures existed to deliver devolved services to communities. Managers considered that specialist staff in smaller authorities might suffer from a loss of peer and management support and would have less opportunity to develop expertise across a broad range of criminal justice work.

MONITORING

Whilst significant progress had been made in most authorities to monitor the quality of services, less emphasis had been placed upon the development of methods to evaluate services, in particular one-to-one work with offenders. In addition, difficulties had been encountered by some authorities in monitoring additional requirements to probation orders and ensuring that specialist agencies were meeting the National Standards in respect of enforcement.

Systems for monitoring and evaluating the effectiveness of prison-based social work services were thought by Main Consultation Group interviewees and managers to be less well developed.

Interviewees acknowledged that the delay in fully implementing the National Core Data System (NCDS) had hindered local planning and a national review of policy implementation. However, steps had been taken to review the system. The delay in publication of Scottish Office criminal justice statistics and results of inspections was considered by managers to have reduced their value in the local planning process.

Main Consultation Group respondents identified a need for the development of a strategic overview of policy and priorities but acknowledged that the Group did not meet sufficiently frequently to undertake a rigorous review of policy implementation at a national level. Some members suggested that either the Group should be reconvened or a separate taskforce should be established.

CONCLUSION

The policy was not fully implemented at the local level by the time of the research, for example, in relation to effective formal liaison between senior social work management and sheriffs, or the availability and quality of services.

This was partly due to the fact that the research was conducted in the early stages of implementation. However, the effectiveness of policy implementation at the national level impacted on policy implementation at the local level. Certain aspects of implementation at the national level facilitated local policy implementation:

- The involvement of key stakeholders in the preparation of the National Standards.
- The National Standards encouraged greater specialisation which resulted in improved quality of services.
- The national planning process enhanced local strategic planning.

Other aspects of national implementation hindered local implementation:

- Not all services are 100 per cent funded, which hindered development of these services and the development of a comprehensive approach to planning and service delivery.
- Sufficient funding was not made available to provide the full range

and level of specialist services required to meet the courts' needs.

- Early strategic planning procedures were not found to be totally effective and these have since been revised.

- The delay in establishing an effective National Core Data System and delays in feedback of national statistics and findings of inspections hindered reviews of the level of national and local policy implementation. However, the NCDS is presently being reviewed.

The full report of the study is *Social Work and Criminal Justice Volume 3: The National and Local Context*, Louise Brown, Liz Levy and Gill McIvor (1998).

SENTENCER DECISION MAKING

INTRODUCTION

The purpose of this study is to examine the impact of the policy on sentencer decision making by providing results which will enable:

- an assessment of the impact of arrangements for the implementation of the National Standards on sentencers' use of non-custodial disposals;

- an assessment of the relationship between sentencers' perceptions of decision making and local practice;

- an assessment of the impact of local liaison arrangements on shrieval decision making.

The findings are based on national sentencing statistics, interviews with sheriffs and social workers and on the results of a content analysis of 212 social enquiry reports (SERs) prepared in the study areas.

THE IMPACT OF THE POLICY ON THE USE OF CUSTODY

The judiciary are bound by legislation, not social work criminal justice policy. However, the policy is intended to improve the quality and availability of community based court disposals and the quality of SERs which assist sentencer decision making. The policy can therefore have an indirect impact on sentencing decisions.

The analysis of Scottish Office criminal justice statistics identified a slight increase in the use of custody since the introduction of the policy in 1991 which is contrary to the expectations of the policy. A reduction in the use of short custodial sentences and a slight increase in the use of probation for younger offenders since 1991 was identified and is consistent with policy objectives. However, there are many factors which can influence sentencing trends, such as an increase in the incidence of more serious offences, and thus it is difficult to isolate the impact of the policy from other factors.

The findings of this study have identified a range of factors which can influence sentencers' decisions to impose a custodial rather than a community based disposal: characteristics of the offence; characteristics of the offender; the quality of SERs; the availability of services; and the credibility of community based disposals. Sheriffs indicated that they had a fundamental concern with public interest and safety.

Characteristics of the Offence

Sheriffs indicated that the gravity of the offence was a main consideration in borderline cases. They said that they would tend to impose a custodial sentence for serious offences where there was a need to protect the public; community service for serious offences where that need was absent; and probation for less serious offences (and where the SER identified a problem which could be addressed through probation and the offender was willing to co-operate).

In some areas sheriffs indicated that they would impose a custodial sentence as a deterrent for certain types of offence whose incidence had increased. However, at the individual level, social workers thought that probation might be more successful in reducing the risk of re-offending in some of these cases.

Characteristics of the Offender

Factors relating to the offender which influenced sheriffs' decisions included: the risk of their re-offending; their motivation to stop offending; the existence of a problem which could be addressed through probation; their willingness to co-operate; whether they were repeat offenders; and their previous experience of a community based disposal. Sheriffs stated that they tended to use custody for repeat offenders as a last resort after community based disposals had been considered or previously tried.

Sheriffs reported that they looked to the SER to provide information and assessments about the offender and that these influenced their decision. Thus it is important that SERs provide sentencers with the information which they require.

Quality of SERs

Although sheriffs were generally satisfied with the quality of reports, the reports in the study sample did not always provide the key information which sheriffs sought (such as the pattern of offending and risk of re-offending), nor did they fully meet the more extensive requirements of the National Standards. The reasons provided by social workers for certain information not being presented included: the information may have been obtained but was not deemed relevant; pressure of work and administrative delays; delays in accessing other agencies; problems in accessing a full list of previous convictions; and problems in obtaining full details of the offence. The latter hindered the social worker's assessment of the offender's attitude to the offence and thus the offender's level of commitment as a potential probationer. Social workers reported that if they had to rely on the offender's version alone, there was a danger that their assessment for a community based disposal could become inappropriate and viewed by sheriffs as unrealistic. In such cases, their recommendation would be unlikely to be followed.

Although court social workers and social work managers acknowledged that there had been an improvement in the quality of SERs since the introduction of the National Standards, they recognised that there was scope for further improvements, for example, by authors taking a more analytic approach rather than being descriptive. It was found that social work departments in the study areas were committed to monitoring and improving the quality of SERs.

Sixty-five per cent of the SER recommendations in the study sample were followed. There was no difference in the level of "missing" information (in respect of the requirements of the National Standards) between reports where the recommendation was accepted or rejected. Most sheriffs said that they would tend to follow a recommendation if it was realistic, was based on the body of the report and took into account the gravity of the offence. However, as social workers had difficulty in accessing full details of the offence, assessments of the gravity of the offence and the presentation of a realistic recommendation were problematic.

Availability of Services

One of the policy objectives was to increase the quantity of specialist services and some were established in the study areas shortly after the policy was introduced in 1991. Despite this, social workers in each area and some sheriffs identified gaps in the range and quantity of provision of specialist services which, sheriffs said, could influence their use of custody. The number of places available on specialist initiatives was relatively small compared to the total number of persons convicted in each court.

Credibility of Community based Court Disposals

Most sheriffs reported that community service continued to be viewed as a credible disposal and that probation had achieved greater credibility since the introduction of the policy. Although Scottish Office statistics demonstrated a slight increase in the use of probation since 1991, the study of probation in this programme found that probation supervision in the study areas had not fully met the National Standards by summer 1995.

Some sheriffs indicated that they would welcome more detailed feedback on the success of orders imposed on "high risk" offenders than that supplied by completion reports. (Some sheriffs said that they might prefer to impose a deferred sentence than probation for 'high risk' cases as they were then able to retain control over the offender by requesting bi-monthly reports.)

Feedback to sentencers on the success of community based court disposals is an important factor in increasing the credibility of these disposals for "high risk" offenders. This can be achieved by providing sentencers with more detailed completion reports on individual "'high risk" cases and by providing detailed local and national assessments of the success of community-based disposals for "high risk" cases. The main forum for providing information on success of community-based disposals is formal liaison meetings between the local social work department and the judiciary.

THE IMPACT OF THE POLICY ON LIAISON

Informal liaison with court social workers, designed to deal with day-to-day problems as they arise, was said by both sheriffs and court social workers to be operating well and to have improved as a result of the appointment of specific court social workers. The National Standards also encourage the establishment of formal liaison meetings between sheriffs and the social work department to discuss strategic issues such as the amount and range of service provision and the information required by sentencers about the outcome of disposals. However, it was found that formal liaison meetings where such issues were discussed, tended not to take place in the study areas. It was suggested that feedback of information to sentencers is required to reduce the uncertainty about the effectiveness of new penal policies before changes in sentencing outcomes become apparent.

However, the study on the national and local context within this programme found that social work departments may not, at the time of the research, have been in a position to provide information on the success of community based disposals, as local and national management information systems had not been fully operational.

CONCLUSION

It is evident that, by the end of the research fieldwork (summer 1995), the policy had not been fully implemented in relation to: the availability and quality of community based services; the quality of SERs; effective formal liaison arrangements; and the feedback of information on the success of community based disposals. It is thus perhaps not surprising that the policy objective of reducing the use of custody had not been achieved by the end of 1994. However, it is acknowledged that sentencing trends can be influenced by factors other than policy implementation.

It is encouraging to note that, although the research covered the early stages of policy implementation and that further improvements could be made, significant progress had been achieved and there was some indication that the use of probation in the study areas had increased.

The full report of the study is *Social Work and Criminal Justice Volume 4: Sentencer Decision Making*, Louise Brown and Liz Levy (1998).

PAROLE BOARD DECISION MAKING

INTRODUCTION

This study examines the impact of arrangements for implementing the policy on Parole Board decision-making including the impact of: social work parole reports; the quality of prison and community-based social work services; and liaison arrangements.

The research is based on: observation of six Parole Board meetings held between January and March 1994; detailed analysis of all cases considered at the meetings (311 cases which are representative of the range of cases with which the Board deals); analysis of a sample of 68 prison social work reports and 63 home circumstances reports, drawn from the parole dossiers of cases considered at the meetings from each of four prison units (one prison unit was selected from each study site to reflect a range of units); semi-structured interviews with four members of the Parole Board for Scotland and four prison social workers; and a group interview conducted with community based social workers from each study site.

SOCIAL WORK PAROLE REPORTS AND DECISION MAKING

Information Requirements of the Board

Parole Board interviewee responses indicate that there was a high level of correspondence between the Parole Board's expectations of both prison social work and home circumstances reports and the requirements of the National Standards. A key concern of the Board was that the authors of prison social work and home circumstances reports should collaborate over the preparation of reports and that the two social work reports should provide a seamless web of information in respect of release plans and risk assessments.

All but one of the Parole Board interviewees were generally satisfied with the prison social work reports which they received. However interviewees considered that the overall quality of home circumstances reports was less good, with two Parole Board interviewees commenting that home circumstances reports were often cursory, giving little indication that they were based on verified sources of information nor that they had been prepared collaboratively with the author of the prison social work report.

Quality of Information in Reports

The information provided in both prison social work and home circumstances reports in the sample suggests that the Board does not always receive reports which fully meet its requirements. None of the reports in the sample fully met the National Standards and only 27 per cent of prison social work reports and 21 per cent of home circumstances reports indicated that they had been prepared on a collaborative basis.

Prison social work reports mainly indicated and assessed: the prisoner's personal circumstances; their response to imprisonment; and attitude towards the offence. Less well covered were the prisoner's attitude towards their sentence and attitudes towards release plans. Just over one half (35) of prison social work reports included an assessment of risk of re-offending.

Areas well covered in home circumstances reports were: background information, especially in relation to accommodation; family attitudes towards the prisoner, and the environment to which the prisoner was to return. However, less than half the reports indicated and assessed: the prisoner's overall level of needs; the suitability of specialist resources to meet those needs; family attitude towards social work supervision; and an assessment of risk factors.

Social Work Views on Reports

Social work interviewee responses highlight a number of reasons as to why reports may fall short of National Standards' requirements. Both prison and community based social work interviewees indicated that they did not always have access to information which would enable them to make the types of assessment required by the National Standards. Most found it difficult to access verified information about the prisoner's criminal history and the nature of the current offence and this created difficulties when making assessments of risk of re-offending. Prison social work interviewee responses also indicate that workloads may have impacted adversely on the extent to which they could implement the standards.

Both prison and community based social workers identified elements of reports for which each considered that the other should take lead responsibility, in particular the development of release plans. (The National Standards require both prison social work and home circumstances reports to indicate the suitability of specialist resources and programmes in the community.) Prison social workers did not consider that they were best placed to assess the suitability of community-based resources for the prisoner whereas community based social workers did not consider that they had sufficient information about the prisoner in order to assess their needs.

Use of Information: Decision making Practice

Although the quality of the report sample indicates that social workers do not always provide reports which meet the Board's expectations, poor quality of information was only an *explicit* factor in a minority of decisions during the observation period. Three decisions out of a total 290 relevant decisions (this excludes decisions made on cases referred for consideration of recall for which no social work reports were available) were deferred to await a more detailed prison social work report with a further five deferred to give community based social workers time to prepare better researched reports.

SOCIAL WORK SERVICES AND DECISION MAKING

Specialist Community based Services

Both Parole Board and social work interviewees considered that National Standards implementation had resulted in the proliferation of certain community-based services, especially addiction counselling. Other services were believed to be markedly less well developed, in particular supported accommodation and services for mentally disordered offenders. The observed decision making patterns indicate however that demand (as evidenced by the nature of additional requirements inserted into licences by the Board) for supported accommodation placements and psychological services was relatively low. By contrast services for which there was greatest demand (such as alcohol counselling) were the most prolific.

Supervision of Licencees

Parole Board interviewees commented that they often lacked information about the content and process of statutory supervision, particularly in relation to parolees. This made it difficult for them to assess whether policy implementation had resulted in improved quality of supervision. Nevertheless, a general view was that quality of supervision was likely to impact on a licencee's willingness to adhere to their licence conditions. However, interviewees considered that there was little that social workers could do to prevent re-offending. This contrasts with the model of social work practice in the National Standards, which is premised on the belief that supervision which provides the requisite balance of care and control can impact positively on offending behaviour.

Prison based Social Work Services

A general view of both Parole Board and prison social work interviewees was that prison social work services had improved since the implementation of *Continuity Through Co-operation* (a national framework of policy and practice guidance for social work in prisons, The Scottish Office Social Work Services Group/Scottish Prison Service

1989) with social workers now undertaking more offence-focused work. Nevertheless, interviewees still considered that there were variations in the range and quality of social work services in different prison establishments. Key gaps in services were identified as: relationship counselling, anger management counselling; and services for gamblers. The uneven nature of service provision was attributed to poor strategic planning on the part of some local authorities and to under-resourcing.

Both Parole Board and prison social work interviewees highlighted the need for prison units to develop a network of services, supplied by both social work and other specialist agencies. Where such a network existed, this was felt to enhance the effectiveness of the social work contribution.

Impact of Community based Services on Parole Board Decision making

Parole Board interviewees did not consider that arrangements for implementing the policy had impacted on their decision-making practice. Both the interview and observation data confirm that the nature or quality of community based social work services did not feature amongst the principal factors which the Board took into account when making decisions in the majority of cases. This limits the impact of a policy aimed at encouraging earlier release on licence by improving the quality of statutory supervision.

Determinate Sentence Cases

For determinate sentence cases, risk of re-offending was the main factor which the Board took into account. Key indicators of risk were identified by Parole Board interviewees as: the nature and circumstances of the current offence; the number and pattern of previous convictions; the extent to which the offender had addressed their offending behaviour and any related problems; the level of support the offender would have on release; and plans for managing time in the community.

However, the observed decision making patterns indicate that in the *majority* of cases where the Board considered that a prisoner had not made efforts to address their offending *during time spent in custody*, the Board attached *less weight* to constructive release plans in their assessment of re-offending risk. Where the Parole Board perceived a prisoner to be low risk they recommended them for parole or a forward release date. High risk prisoners by contrast were generally not released.

Analysis of the decision making patterns identified only 39 (18%) out of 216 determinate sentence cases for which there was evidence that social work services were an important consideration in the decision that was made. However, a high proportion of these cases was considered to be at a low risk of re-offending or had features which the Board confirmed in interview to be indicative of low risk, *in addition* to the identified social work resource. As cases with such low risk features were generally recommended for release, this suggests that the availability of social work services had a *contributory* but not necessarily a *pivotal* role to play in the positive outcomes for these cases.

However, in 13 of these 39 cases, all identified as being at high risk of re-offending and potentially dangerous (mainly convicted of violent and sex offences), the availability of social work services was a crucial element in the decision made. All of these cases were at their final review for parole purposes and the input of community based social work resources was considered essential as a means of risk management. Parole Board interviewees confirmed that these were the most difficult type of cases on which to make decisions. Where release on licence was recommended (in 11 of these cases), the Board's aim was to ensure that the prisoner would return to a controlled environment for a short period. The role of social work under these circumstances was less rehabilitative and more a means of keeping track of offenders.

Targeting resources and standards on the community based element of throughcare services is unlikely to encourage the Parole Board to release *greater* numbers of determinate sentence prisoners on licence at an *earlier* stage unless the Board changes its perspective on the context in which reduction in the risk of re-offending should take place. This would require the Board to accept that risk reduction should be effected in a community-based rather than custodial setting.

Indeterminate Sentence Cases

For indeterminate sentence prisoners the principal focus of decision-making was progress in custody. Key measures of progress were identified as: response to testing, for example on home leaves or in open conditions; and progress in addressing significant problems. The focus on change in custody meant that community based social work services did not feature in any of the decisions made in relation to this type of case.

A further impediment to policy impact may be the stage at which indeterminate sentence cases are referred to the Board. Release on licence for most cases will be at least one year away from the time at which the case is considered by the Board and dependent upon the successful completion of a pre-release programme. Detailed planning for release may not begin until the prisoner has been recommended for provisional release (as confirmed in a number of prison social work reports for indeterminate sentence cases in the report sample).

Impact of Prison Social Work Services on Decision making

The Board's focus on change during time spent in custody (both in respect of progress for indeterminate sentence cases and reduction in the level of risk of re-offending for determinate sentence cases) highlights the scope for high quality and effective prison based social work services to impact positively on parole decisions. However, Parole Board interviewees recognised that the impact of prison social work on the behaviour and attitudes of prisoners was often dependent on the motivation of the individual prisoner to change. Prisoners are not obliged to undertake counselling during time spent in custody and absence of motivation to change means that they will not generally be accepted on specialist programmes. In this respect, expansions in the range and quality of prison social work services may provide greater *opportunities* for prisoners to address their problems, but this will only impact on the Board's decision making practice where prisoners *themselves* choose to make use of these opportunities.

LIAISON

When asked about liaison Parole Board members had little to say. Liaison between the Parole Board and officials from SWSG and SPS generally took place when officials attended the Parole Board's General Purposes meetings. While some were satisfied with these arrangements others felt that the Board required to be consulted more often about the development of policy.

CONCLUSION

Throughcare services were identified at Phase One of the research programme as being the most poorly developed element of social work criminal justice services. Interviewee responses indicate that the aspects of throughcare which impact on the parole process are still unevenly developed.

A key aim of Central Government is to facilitate common ownership of the policy in order that key criminal justice decision makers develop shared perspectives on, and have greater confidence in, the role of community based social work services in risk management. It would appear from the research findings of this study that common ownership does not as yet extend to the Parole Board.

The full report of the study is *Social Work and Criminal Justice Volume 5: Parole Board Decision Making*, Lesley McAra, (1998a).

PROBATION

INTRODUCTION

This study examines the process and outcomes of probation supervision following the introduction of 100 per cent funding and National Standards. In examining the process and outcomes of probation supervision in Scotland it seeks to describe the characteristics of probationers; to document the services offered by supervising social workers and the framework within which they are provided; and to examine the effectiveness of probation supervision in meeting probationers' needs and reducing the risk of further offending behaviour.

In three of the study authorities - Bruce, Scott and Wallace - the research focused upon probation cases held by two social work teams. In the fourth area - Burns - the focus was upon the work of a single team. The research focused upon probation cases closed between 1 July 1994 and 30 April 1995. Information was obtained, in the main, from social work case files, from questionnaires completed by supervising social workers in individual cases and from interviews with probationers.

CHARACTERISTICS OF THE SAMPLE

The total sample consisted of 155 offenders sentenced to probation across the four study areas. The majority of orders had been imposed by the sheriff court under summary proceedings. Just under half contained additional requirements, with the nature of these requirements tending to reflect the availability of services in the study areas. Eighty-two per cent of probationers were male and just under half were between 16 and 20 years of age. Around half the sample had six or more previous convictions when made subject to probation and just under three-fifths had received their orders for offences involving dishonesty. Thirty-eight per cent of probationers were believed by SER authors to have been at risk of a custodial sentence. Family problems, drug and alcohol abuse and mental health problems featured prominently in SERs. Offending was most often attributed to alcohol or drug abuse, though in a fifth of cases offenders were said to have been motivated by financial gain and in a similar proportion of cases offending was described as opportunistic or impulsive. In recommending probation to the courts, social workers generally referred to the potential offered by probation to address offending behaviour or behaviour associated with offending, to provide help with practical problems or support of a more general kind, or to capitalise upon the offender's motivation to change.

Differences Between Research Sites

Probationers in Bruce were more likely to have been ordained to appear for sentence and were less likely to have received probation for offences involving dishonesty. Bruce contained a higher proportion of female offenders and a slightly lower proportion of young offenders than the other two areas. Probationers in Bruce had fewest previous convictions and custodial sentences, were more likely to be first offenders and were less likely to have previous experience of community-based social work disposals. They were less likely to have been considered by the SER author as being at risk of custody but were more likely to have additional requirements recommended to the court.

By contrast, probationers in Wallace had been sentenced for a higher number of offences, had most previous convictions and had served a higher average number of previous custodial sentences. Wallace contained the lowest proportion of first offenders and the highest proportion of persistent offenders. Probationers in Wallace were most likely to be considered at risk of custody and were most likely to be breached.

Differences Between Types of Offender

Young offenders were more likely than adults to have been recommended for and to receive a probation order with additional requirements, to have been given probation for an offence involving dishonesty, to have been considered at risk of custody and to have been breached. They were more often than adults described in SERs as having family problems and problems related to low educational achievement. Offending by young probationers was more often described as impulsive or opportunistic, as a response to boredom or as having occurred under the influence of offending peers, and they were more likely to be recommended for probation as a means of obtaining help with employment. By contrast, alcohol abuse and medical or mental health problems were more likely to feature among adult offenders and their offending was more likely to be linked to alcohol abuse or emotional pressure. Probation was more likely to be recommended for adults as a means of addressing the abuse of alcohol or drugs.

In comparison with first or early offenders, persistent offenders were more likely to have additional requirements recommended and attached to their probation orders. They were more likely to have been sentenced for a main offence involving dishonesty, were more often considered at risk of custody and were more likely to be breached. Peer group pressure was more often invoked in explanations of offending by first or early offenders and probation was more likely to be recommended for this category of offender as a means of addressing relationship and financial problems. Alcohol and drug abuse more often featured in explanations of offending by persistent offenders and they were more likely to be recommended for probation to address offending behaviour and drug abuse and to access help in relation to housing and general support.

Female probationers were less likely than males to have additional requirements recommended and attached to their orders. They were slightly older than men, less likely to be single and more likely to have dependent children living in the same household. Women had fewer previous convictions, were more often first offenders and were less likely to have previously served a custodial sentence. Whilst men and women were equally likely to have received probation for offences involving dishonesty, women's offences typically involved theft and fraud while men's offences involved housebreaking and car theft. Women were less likely to be breached and were more likely to have their probation orders discharged early on the grounds of satisfactory progress having been made. Women were more often identified as having mental health or emotional problems. Their offending was more likely to be explained in terms of financial gain or as a response to emotional stress and they were more likely than men to be recommended for probation as a means of accessing support of a general kind. Male probationers were more often described as having problems relating to alcohol abuse. Their offending was more likely to be linked to alcohol, to be described as opportunistic or impulsive or to have been in response to boredom. Probation was more likely to be recommended for male than female probationers to address offending behaviour and alcohol abuse.

THE PROBATION PROCESS

Contacts with Social Workers

The process of probation supervision was examined in 112 cases. The National Standard which stipulates that probationers should first be seen within one week of the order being made was met in 67 per cent of cases; the requirement of at least eight contacts in the first three months was met in 44 per cent of cases; that requiring at least two home visits in the first three months in 47 per cent of cases; and the timing of initial reviews in 51 per cent of cases. With the exception of home visits, the standards were consistently less often met in Bruce than in the other study areas. The lower number of reviews in Wallace appeared to be attributable to the higher percentage of breached orders in that area.

Action Plans

Services Offered

Action plans were present in all but three probation case files. Offending behaviour, personal relationships and employment featured most often in action plans and in the services offered to probationers. The majority of services were delivered on an individual basis and most were provided by the supervising social worker. Other individuals or agencies were most likely to be involved in the provision of services relating to employment, alcohol, drugs and health issues. The objectives most often identified in case files focused upon offending, employment, alcohol and drugs. Action plans and services provided varied according to the characteristics of probationers.

Differences Between Research Sites

The areas of work identified in action plans and the services provided to probationers varied across the research areas. Action plans and services provided to offenders in Bruce were less likely to include reference to offending behaviour, alcohol abuse or financial problems and were more likely to focus upon relationships, use of leisure time and physical or mental health.

The primary objectives and services provided to probationers in Scott were more often addressed to offending behaviour, drug and alcohol use, financial problems and social skills.

Action plans in Wallace were least likely to include reference to the probationer's use of leisure time, and work undertaken with probationers in this area was less likely to focus upon accommodation, employment and drugs. The primary objectives in work with probationers in Wallace were broadly similar to those in Scott, focusing on offending, employment, alcohol and drugs. The apparent mismatch between probation objectives and services provided in Wallace is likely to be attributable to the high breach rate which prevented much work from being undertaken in a significant proportion of cases.

THE OUTCOMES OF PROBATION

Around three-fifths of objectives appeared to have been achieved in full or to a significant degree though this was true of only 14 per cent of objectives identified in respect of probationers who were breached. Objectives relating to offending behaviour appeared to have been achieved completely or to a significant extent in 56 per cent of cases, those relating to employment or accommodation appeared least often to have been achieved. Objectives were less likely to have been achieved in Wallace (43 per cent) than in Bruce (69 per cent) or Scott (71 per cent), but this was attributable to the higher proportion of breaches in that area. With breaches excluded, objectives appeared more often to have been achieved in Scott (85 per cent) than in Bruce (68 per cent) or Wallace (69 per cent).

Probation objectives were more often achieved in full or to a significant extent with adult offenders, though much of this difference could be accounted for by the higher proportion of young offenders who were breached. Objectives were more likely to be achieved with first or early offenders than with persistent offenders even when "successful" orders alone were considered. When successful orders alone were considered, objectives were more often achieved in whole or to a significant degree in respect of probationers sentenced for offences involving dishonesty. Objectives were more often achieved with female probationers, this difference being accounted for partly, but not entirely, by the lower breach rate among women.

Fifty-nine per cent of orders were completed in full, 14 per cent were discharged early and 25 per cent were breached. The highest breach rate and the highest proportions of probationers who received one or more formal warnings were found in Wallace, while probation orders in Bruce were more likely than in the other areas to have been terminated through an application for early discharge. Just under half the breach applications resulted from the probationer's conviction for a further offence and just over half of all breaches resulted in the imposition of a custodial sentence. Overall, just under a third of probationers were convicted of or charged with a further offence while on probation: the proportion was highest in Wallace and identical in Bruce and Scott, despite the fact that probationers in Scott might have been assumed, on the basis of their previous criminal histories, to present a higher risk of re-offending than in Bruce.

SOCIAL WORKERS' VIEWS OF THE EFFECTIVENESS OF PROBATION

Objectives

Addressing offending and drug use, providing the probationer with practical support, getting the probationer through the order and addressing attitudes or behaviour associated with offending were the objectives of supervision most commonly identified by social workers in the 98 cases for which questionnaires were completed. The greatest progress was thought to be made towards achieving objectives concerned with personal relationships, offending and successful completion of the order. Around a third of probationers were said to have been very motivated to address their offending and just over a quarter were thought highly motivated to address other problems. Three-fifths of probationers were said to have responded positively to probation.

Likelihood of Re-offending

Forty per cent of probationers were considered unlikely to re-offend while in 17 per cent of cases re-offending was thought very likely. Perceived risk of re-offending was inversely related to probationers' motivation, their response to probation and the extent to which offending-related objectives had been achieved. Probationers were assessed as very likely to re-offend because their attitudes, behaviour or circumstances were unchanged. In discussing probationers who were considered unlikely to re-offend, social workers made reference to their motivation to avoid further offending, improvements or stability in their personal circumstances and the acquisition of personal skills.

Just under three-quarters of probationers were considered less likely to re-offend since being placed on probation. Probation was believed to have had some positive impact upon the risk of re-offending in 68 per cent of cases in the sample.

Differences Between Research Sites

The objectives identified by social workers varied across the research sites. Probation objectives were least likely to be achieved in Wallace and probationers in Wallace were more often thought than in other areas to present a continued risk of re-offending.

Probationers in Bruce were less likely to be considered at risk of further offending and were more likely to be said to have demonstrated a reduction in risk while subject to probation than those in other areas. Social workers in Bruce appeared to place as much emphasis upon offending behaviour than did those in the other study areas even though offending featured less often in this area in the reasons for recommending probation, in action plans, in the services provided to probationers and in the objectives derived from an analysis of case files. The pattern of findings suggests that tackling offending may often have been an implicit objective in Bruce, which was addressed indirectly through attention to other areas.

Differences Between Types of Offender

Young offenders were considered to have been less motivated to address their offending and other problems and less likely to have shown a positive response to probation. They were more often thought to present a risk of continued offending and were less likely to have demonstrated a reduction in risk of re-offending since being made subject to probation.

Probation objectives were less likely to have been achieved with persistent offenders, who were more often thought not to have been motivated to address their offending and other problems. Persistent offenders were less often said to have demonstrated a positive response to probation and were more often thought to present a risk of continued offending. Persistent offenders were, however, equally likely to have shown a reduced risk of re-offending since being placed on probation.

Women were more often said to have been motivated to address their offending behaviour and other problems, and were more often thought to have shown a positive response to probation supervision, while men were considered more likely to re-offend. These differences appeared, however, to be attributable to the differing characteristics of male and female probationers in the sample.

PROBATIONERS' EXPERIENCES AND VIEWS OF PROBATION

Objectives of the Order and Motivation

Most of the 65 probationers who were interviewed recognised that one of the main purposes of probation was to address offending behaviour and just over half suggested that it was also intended to provide help with problems. The majority stressed the importance of being motivated to change and willing to contribute to the process for probation to be effective. Most probationers were unclear about the existence of an action plan, though they were aware of what the social worker considered to be the main issues in the case and were generally in accordance with the social worker's definition of the problem areas to be addressed. Offending behaviour and drug or alcohol problems were most often mentioned by probationers as areas which should be worked on during probation. Three-quarters of probationers indicated that they had been motivated to address their problems when placed on probation; however, in agreement with social workers' views, younger offenders were less likely than adult probationers to be motivated in this respect.

Content of Supervision

Just under half the probationers thought that the length of their order had been about right while a third believed it to have been too long. Most believed that the frequency of contact with their social worker was about right though a few would have preferred more or less frequent contact, depending upon their circumstances. Probationers identified help with practical or emotional problems, having someone to talk to, and referral to/liaison with other agencies as of most benefit to them. Most believed that the help they received from their social workers was adequate though two-fifths would have valued additional help of a practical or supportive kind. The features of probation which probationers found least helpful were the location or frequency of appointments and the possibility of breach. The relationship established with the social worker appeared to be a significant aspect of probation supervision. Those features of the social worker's approach which probationers found most helpful were openness and approachability combined with an ability to influence circumstances and help the probationer to better understand his/her situation and behaviour.

When asked what they had hoped to achieve while on probation, probationers most often cited avoidance of further offending (in just under three-fifths of cases) followed by employment/education, addressing drug use, obtaining a more stable lifestyle, personal development, addressing alcohol use and accommodation. The majority of probationers reported that they had discussed offending behaviour in some detail during their probation order. Those who had attended probation groups or intensive probation programmes generally found such approaches to be stimulating and challenging.

Risk of Re-offending

Most probationers believed that it was unlikely that they would re-offend, though further offending was thought more likely by younger probationers. Compared with when they were placed on probation, over three-quarters of probationers considered themselves to be less at risk of re-offending and the majority of this group believed that probation had played some part in reducing this risk. Other factors which were said to have impacted positively upon their risk of re-offending included their own motivation to avoid offending and its consequences and improvements in their personal circumstances.

Overall, most probationers believed that their experience on probation had been worthwhile. While a quarter thought that they had gained nothing from probation, the remainder cited benefits such as resolving their problems, gaining self confidence, motivation or self respect, learning self control and having "time out" to reflect on or change their situation. Some wanted not just supervision but an element of control to provide structure in their lives which had been absent in the past.

CONCLUSION

There were area differences in policy implementation which, it is suggested, could be attributable to organisational factors at the local level. More specifically, National Standards were least often met in Bruce, there was less evidence of clear targeting and gate-keeping and probation practice appeared more closely aligned to a traditional welfare model which places greater emphasis upon probationers' problems and less on their offending behaviour. This, it is suggested, may have resulted from the existence of generic management arrangements and the absence of systematic monitoring in that area.

It is concluded that the research presents a generally optimistic picture of probation practice in Scotland. The framework provided by the National Standards appears on the whole to provide an appropriate structure within which offending behaviour and other issues can be addressed. The policy initiative appears to have succeeded in large measure in re-focusing probation practice such as to enhance its emphasis upon tackling offending behaviour and in so doing increase the effectiveness, in the short term at least, of probation supervision. Some managers, however, believed that further progress could still be made in relation to the development of more imaginative approaches to work with probationers, including the use of groupwork and modular programmes, especially with younger offenders with whom probation appeared to be less effective.

The full report of the study is *Social Work and Criminal Justice Volume 6: Probation*, Gill McIvor and Monica Barry (1998).

COMMUNITY BASED THROUGHCARE

INTRODUCTION

This study examines the process and outcome of community-based throughcare services following the introduction of 100 per cent funding and National Standards. It seeks to describe the characteristics of ex-prisoners subject to different throughcare arrangements; to document the services offered by community based social workers and the framework within which they are provided; and to examine the effectiveness of community based throughcare in addressing ex-prisoners' needs and assisting in their resettlement in the community.

In three of the four study authorities throughcare cases for inclusion in the sample were drawn from across the region as a whole. This step was taken to maximise the number of cases which could be identified within a given period of time. In the fourth area the focus was upon throughcare cases dealt with by two area teams in the district, including those held by a dedicated throughcare project (funded by the Urban Renewal Unit) which offered a service to offenders from areas of priority treatment (APTs) across the district.

The total possible sample consisted of all throughcare cases (parole, statutory aftercare and voluntary aftercare) which closed between 1 July 1994 and 30 April 1995 and which related to prisoners who had been released from custody since April 1992 (when the National Standards for throughcare came into effect). Also included were life licencees who, though still subject to statutory supervision, had been released from custody since April 1992. Information was obtained in the main from social work files, from questionnaires completed by social workers in individual cases and from interviews with ex-prisoners.

CHARACTERISTICS OF THE SAMPLE

More than two-thirds of the sample of 60 ex-prisoners were subject to parole and just over half of this group had additional requirements attached to their licences by the Parole Board. Additional requirements most frequently related to drug or alcohol counselling, residence and treatment for sexual offending. Most of the additional requirements in respect of drug counselling pertained to offenders who had been sentenced for offences involving drugs. Parolees in Bruce were most likely to have additional requirements attached to their licences. Most parole licences were for durations of up to 12 months. The average period on licence was highest in Scott and lowest in Bruce.

The average length of determinate sentence imposed was 40 months. Ex-prisoners in receipt of voluntary assistance on release had served, on average, shorter sentences than those subject to statutory supervision.

The majority of the sample were males over 20 years of age. Life licencees were older, on average, than other groups of former prisoners.

The majority of ex-prisoners had one or more previous convictions and just over half had previously served a custodial sentence. Just under a third of prisoners in receipt of community-based throughcare had been subject to supervision through the children's hearing system and more than a third had previous experience of community based social work disposals. Ex-prisoners in receipt of voluntary assistance had more extensive criminal histories, on average, than did those who were subject to statutory supervision on release.

THE THROUGHCARE PROCESS

Contacts with Social Workers

Twenty-nine ex-prisoners had received a visit from their community based social worker while in custody and in 31 cases supervising social workers had established contact with prisoners' families, usually in connection with the preparation of a home circumstances report for the Parole Board. Most ex-prisoners on statutory supervision were seen by their supervising social worker within 24 hours of their release. Ex-prisoners who received voluntary assistance made contact, on average, six weeks after being released from custody.

Prisoners subject to statutory supervision had more contacts with their social workers than did those in receipt of voluntary assistance. Ex-prisoners in Scott had more office contacts with their social workers in the first three months of supervision and had slightly more contacts overall during this period than did those in the other areas. National Standards with respect to the frequency of contact in the first three months and the date of initial contact with statutory throughcare cases were more often met in Scott than in the other study areas.

Reviews

Formal reviews were held in 29 cases with just over half of these former prisoners having a single review. Initial reviews were conducted, on average, 17 weeks after the prisoner's release. Few reviews resulted in amendments to the objectives of supervision. Reviews in Scott were most likely to be attended by the social worker's first line manager and this was least likely to occur in Wallace.

Objectives and Services Provided

The majority of services provided both at the pre-release stage and following release focused upon practical issues such as accommodation, financial matters and employment. The majority of work was undertaken on a one-to-one basis and, with the exception of employment services and services for offenders with problems related to the use of alcohol or drugs, most work was undertaken by the supervising social workers themselves.

There were some variations in the services provided and objectives pursued across the study areas. Work in Scott, for example, more often focused on employment and accommodation, while the broader aim of re-settling the offender in the community was most prevalent in Bruce and social workers in Wallace were most likely to focus upon offending behaviour.

Accommodation featured most often as an objective with voluntary cases. Work with life licencees was most clearly focused upon practical issues associated with the re-integration of the ex-prisoner in the community, while objectives pursued and services provided in respect of parolees with additional requirements most often focused upon offending behaviour and alcohol and drug abuse, suggesting that this category of ex-prisoner was perceived as presenting the greatest risk of further offending on release.

THE OUTCOMES OF THROUGHCARE

Few ex-prisoners received formal warnings while subject to supervision and only two were recalled to prison as a consequence of further offending; both, significantly in view of the previous argument, were parolees with additional requirements attached to their licences. Eight individuals were reconvicted of offences committed while in receipt of community-based throughcare and one had been charged with an offence allegedly committed during this period. Young offenders were more likely than adults to have been reconvicted and those who were reconvicted had more serious offending histories as evidenced by the number of previous convictions and previous custodial sentences. Voluntary assistance was terminated in most instances because outstanding issues had been addressed or because the ex-prisoner ceased to maintain contact with the social work department.

There was some evidence of an improvement in ex-prisoners' social circumstances - as indicated by changes in living arrangements and employment status - following the period of community based throughcare.

SOCIAL WORKERS' VIEWS OF THE EFFECTIVENESS OF THROUGHCARE

Objectives

Avoiding or addressing offending featured as an objective in just over three-fifths of the 48 cases in which social workers completed questionnaires. This was followed by employment/education, accommodation, helping the offender to re-settle in the community, alcohol and family relationships. Social workers appeared to make greatest progress in relation to alcohol use, the provision of general practical support and helping ex-prisoners to resettle in the community. They had least success in dealing with problematic drug use, helping ex-prisoners to obtain accommodation and providing them with emotional support.

Responses to Throughcare

The majority of ex-prisoners were said by social workers to have been motivated to address their offending and other problems and three-quarters of the sample were believed to have responded positively to throughcare. Factors which were believed by social workers to have adversely affected ex-prisoners' responses to throughcare included the existence of social or personal problems which detracted from the ex-prisoner's ability or willingness to comply; reluctance on the part of the offender to engage with the social worker; the personal characteristics of the offender; and the influence of offending peers. Ex-prisoners' responses to throughcare were believed by their social workers to have been influenced positively by their motivation to avoid further offending and its consequences; by stability in their lives; and by features of the throughcare contact itself - the help received, the relationship established with the social worker or the clear framework provided by a statutory licence.

Likelihood of Re-offending

Two-thirds of ex-prisoners were believed unlikely to re-offend, a quarter were thought fairly likely to re-offend and in one in nine cases further offending was considered very likely. Offenders who were described as highly motivated to address their offending and other problems were least likely to be considered at some risk of committing offences in future. Risk of continued offending was indicated by continued offending during the period on throughcare, by the existence of problematic alcohol or drug use or other factors associated with offending, or by general instability in the ex-prisoners' lives. By contrast, in providing reasons why ex-prisoners were unlikely to re-offend, social workers made reference to the isolated nature of the original offence or the time that had elapsed since its commission; offenders' motivation to avoid offending and its consequences; the stability of the ex-prisoner's circumstances; and improvements in the offender's circumstances since the commission of the original offence.

Forty-four per cent of the sample were considered by their social workers to be less at risk of re-offending compared with when they were released from custody, while in 48 per cent of cases the risk of recidivism was thought not to have changed.

Most offenders whose risk of recidivism was thought not to have changed were not considered to be at risk of further offending. Increased self awareness appeared to be the key factor which distinguished those whose risk of re-offending remained low throughout and those whose risk had decreased since returning to the community. Overall, throughcare was thought to have contributed to a reduced risk of re-offending in approximately 40 per cent of cases in the sample.

EX-PRISONERS' EXPERIENCES AND VIEWS OF THROUGHCARE

Effectiveness of Throughcare

Most of those subject to release on licence had high expectations of the social work support they might receive though seven saw parole as merely a monitoring or surveillance exercise.

Although some of the 31 respondents were able to cite examples of constructive help they had received from prison based social workers, most viewed prison social work input as unhelpful either because social workers were seen as untrustworthy or uninterested or because the insular or detached nature of prison life made prison social workers less effective in liaising with the outside world.

Views were mixed as to the helpfulness of visits in prison from their community based social worker, with some indicating that they would have welcomed more assistance in relation to housing on release. Most ex-prisoners who had had no contact with their community based social worker prior to release would have valued such contact.

Respondents were generally of the view that there was agreement between themselves and their social workers as to what constituted the most pressing issues to address following release. The areas in which the greatest divergence of views was thought to exist were accommodation and offending behaviour: social workers, it was suggested, tended to underestimate the significance of the former and overplay the importance of the latter. Overall, nine ex-prisoners believed that their situation had improved as a direct result of social work advice or intervention but 22 thought that their circumstances had not improved or, if they had, that they themselves had achieved the change on their own.

Risk of Re-offending

Only seven offenders believed that offending might still be a problem which they wanted to address on release. Others felt that offending was an irrelevant issue frequently raised by the social worker, though nine ex-prisoners did not recall having discussed it at all. The majority of ex-prisoners thought it unlikely that they would re-offend and most believed that they were at less of risk of re-offending compared with when they were first released from custody. Throughcare was believed to have had some impact on the likelihood of re-offending by 42 per cent of the sample. Other factors which had impacted positively upon the risk of recidivism included offenders' own motivation to avoid further offending and the significance of family and other personal relationships. More generally, ex-prisoners pointed to increased stability in their lives in areas such as employment or education, social contacts, increased maturity and control over former misuse of alcohol or drugs, issues which had similarly been stressed as significant by social workers.

Around two-thirds believed that their social worker had been helpful overall but just under a third felt that their involvement with social workers was too intrusive and time-consuming. Almost two-thirds of the sample felt they had gained nothing from the experience of throughcare. Just under half would have welcomed more proactive, practical support, particularly in relation to issues such as accommodation and employment.

CONCLUSION

It is concluded that effective pockets of throughcare practice do exist. However, community based throughcare was viewed as less helpful than it might be by released prisoners and was acknowledged by social work managers to be the least well developed of the 100 per cent funded services. What appears to be required to improve the quality and effectiveness of community based throughcare is:

- greater clarity regarding the objectives of throughcare practice (including the distinction between managing risk to the public and addressing offending behaviour);
- a level of resourcing which accurately reflects the requirements of an effective and comprehensive throughcare service;
- a clearer distinction between the role of prison based and community based social work staff in the period prior to release;
- improved communication and co-ordination between prison based and community based social workers;
- a longer time lapse between prisoners' notification of parole being granted and their release date;

- a more consistent emphasis upon the practical needs of prisoners on release.

The full report of the study is *Social Work and Criminal Justice Volume 7: Community Based Throughcare*, Gill McIvor and Monica Barry (1998a).

ANNEX 1

Characteristics of the Study Areas

	Area Type	Court Features	Social Work Organisation	Specialist Services
Scott	Large town bordering urban area	Large court Above national average use of custody, community service and probation. Below average use of fines	Split posts involving child protection and 60% - 80% criminal justice work. Generic middle management	SWD run: Intensive probation; substance misuse. Independent sector: alcohol misuse; mental health
Wallace	City	Large court Above national average use of custody, community service and probation. Below average use of fines	Specialist up to senior management level	SWD run: sex offender; mental health Independent sector: intensive probation; employment; supported accommodation; substance misuse; alcohol misuse
Burns	Large town in rural area	Medium court Below national average use of custody, about average use of community service and fines, above average use of probation	Specialist to middle management level	SWD run: substance misuse. Independent sector: intensive probation; alcohol misuse; domestic violence; supported accommodation; employment
Bruce	Small town in rural area	Small court Below national average use of custody and fines, above average use of community service and probation	Specialist with generic middle management	Independent sector : substance misuse; employment

REFERENCES

Bottoms, A. (1995) The Philosophy and Politics of Punishment and Sentencing in *The Politics of Sentencing Reform*. C.M.V. Clarkson and R. Morgan. Oxford: Clarendon Press.

Brown, L. and Levy, L. (1998) *Social Work and Criminal Justice: Sentencer Decision Making*. Edinburgh: The Stationery Office.

Brown, L., Levy, L. and McIvor, G. (1998) *Social Work and Criminal Justice: The National and Local Context*. Edinburgh: The Stationery Office.

Brown, M. (1996) Serious Offending and the Management of Public Risk in New Zealand: *British Journal of Criminology 36, 1:18-36*.

Creamer, A., Hartley, L. and Williams, Bryan (1992) *The Probation Alternative - A Study of the Impact of Four Enhanced Probation Schemes on Sentencing*. Edinburgh: The Stationery Office Central Research Unit.

Criminal Justice (Scotland) Act 1995.

Criminal Procedure (Scotland) Act 1995.

Curran, J. H. and Chambers, G. A. (1982): *Social Enquiry Reports in Scotland*, Edinburgh: HMSO.

Gelsthorpe, L. and Raynor, P. (1995) Quality and Effectiveness in Probation Officers Reports to Sentencers: *British Journal of Criminology, 35, 2: 188-200*.

Hogarth, J. (1971), *Sentencing: A Human Process*. Toronto: Toronto University Press.

Law Reform (Miscellaneous Provisions) (Scotland) Act 1990.

McAra, L. (1998). *Social Work and Criminal Justice: Early Arrangements*. Edinburgh: The Stationery Office.

McAra, L. (1998a). *Social Work and Criminal Justice: Parole Board Decision Making*. Edinburgh: The Stationery Office.

McIvor, G. and Barry, M. (1998). *Social Work and Criminal Justice: Probation*. Edinburgh: The Stationery Office.

McIvor, G. and Barry, M. (1998a). *Social Work and Criminal Justice: Community Based Throughcare*. Edinburgh: The Stationery Office.

McIvor, G. (1989) *An Evaluative Study of Community Service by Offenders in Scotland*, Social Work Research Centre, University of Stirling.

McIvor, G. (1992) *Reconviction Among Offenders Sentenced to Community Service*, Social Work Research Centre, University of Stirling.

McIvor, G. (1992) *Sentenced to Serve: The Operation and Impact of Community Service by Offenders*, Aldershot: Avebury.

Moody, S. and Tombs, J. (1982)*Prosecution in the Public Interest.* Edinburgh: Scottish Academic Press.

Moore, G. and Wood, C. (1992) *Social Work and Criminal Law in Scotland*. Edinburgh: The Mercat Press.

Nash, M. 2nd Edition (1992) Dangerousness Revisited *International Journal Of The Sociology Of Law*, 20: 337-349.

National Objectives and Standards for Social Work Services in the Criminal Justice System, (1991) The Scottish Office Social Work Services Group.

National Standards for Community Service (1989).

O'Leary, F. (1991). *Summary of the Main Principles Adopted by Central Government in the Preparation of the National Standards Document* (Unpublished).

Palmer, T. (1995) Programmatic and Non-programmatic Aspects of Successful Intervention: New Directions for Research: *Crime and Delinquency* 41, 1: 100-131.

Prisoners and Criminal Proceedings (Scotland) Act 1993.

Raynor, P., Gelsthorpe, L. and Tisi, A. (1995) Quality Assurance, Pre-Sentence Reports and the Probation Service, *British Journal of Social Work*, 25: 483.

Report of the Kilbrandon Committee on Children and Young Persons (Scotland) 1964 Edinburgh: HMSO.

Research Evaluation Strategy Paper, September 1990. Unpublished.

Rumgay, J. (1995) Custodial Decision Making in a Magistrates Court, *British Journal of Criminology*, 35, 2: 201-217.

Social Work (Scotland) Act 1968.

Scottish Prison Service (1990) *Opportunity and Responsibility*, Edinburgh: HMSO.

Scottish Prison Service/SWSG *Continuity Through Co-operation*: February 1990.

Social Work Services Inspectorate (SWSI) (1993) *Social Work Services in the Criminal Justice System: Achieving National Standards*. Edinburgh: The Scottish Office.

Social Work Services Inspectorate (SWSI) (1996) *Helping the Courts Decide*. The Scottish Office.

Social Work Services Inspectorate (SWSI) (1996) *Realistic and Rigorous*. Edinburgh: The Stationery Office.

Social Work Services Inspectorate (SWSI) (1997) *A Positive Penalty*. Edinburgh: The Scottish Office.

Stanley, S. and Murphy, S. (1984) *Inner London Probation Service: Survey of Social Enquiry Reports*. London: Inner London Probation Service.

Printed in Scotland for The Stationery Office Limited
J37711, C9, 2/98, CCN 003808